When Women Pray

ALSO BY T. D. JAKES

When Women Pray

10 Women of the Bible Who
Changed the World through Prayer

T. D. JAKES

New York   Nashville

FaithWords
Hachette Book Group
1290 Avenue of the Americas, New York, NY 10104
faithwords.com
twitter.com/faithwords

First edition: September 2020

FaithWords is a division of Hachette Book Group, Inc. The FaithWords name and logo are trademarks of Hachette Book Group, Inc.

The publisher is not responsible for websites (or their content) that are not owned by the publisher.

The Hachette Speakers Bureau provides a wide range of authors for speaking events. To find out more, go to www.hachettespeakersbureau .com or call (866) 376-6591.

Scripture quotations are taken from the Holy Bible, New International Version®, NIV®. Copyright ©1973, 1978, 1984, 2011 by Biblica, Inc.™ Used by permission of Zondervan. All rights reserved worldwide. www.zondervan.com. The "NIV" and "New International Version" are trademarks registered in the United States Patent and Trademark Office by Biblica, Inc.™

Library of Congress Control Number: 2020938831

ISBNs: 978-1-5460-1559-8 (hardcover), 978-1-5460-1557-4 (ebook), 978-1-5460-1560-4 (large print), 978-1-5460-2949-6 (international)

Printed in the United States of America

LSC-K

10 9 8 7 6 5 4 3 2 1

Contents

Contents

Introduction

She starts the day the same way she has started every day for years. For decades. Lowering her knees to the compacted dirt of her simple quarters, she sits back on her heels and bows her head toward the ground. In the quiet stillness surrounding her, she quiets the racing echoes of her mind. She wants to be ready for this moment—ready to speak and listen, to offer and receive.

Ready to pray.

It's 5:00 a.m. and she has much to accomplish. In an hour she will join the other members of her order for morning mass. That will be a respite. A chance to sit unknown and unrecognized among the rows of worshipers in blue and white habits. A chance to worship. A chance to be filled.

Then it will be time to serve. To give of herself. When mass concludes, she will connect with each visitor in attendance, clasping every offered hand in both of her own, wrinkled fingers squeezing warmly. Next, she will walk the streets of her city to visit the sick and the needy. There is food and medicine to be offered. Comfort as well. Along the way, she will search for those cast aside by the rushing world: the sick, the unstable, the unwanted. She will especially seek out those children whose only shelter is the dusty streets and whose only comfort is the occasional scrap of food from pitying pedestrians.

She will find them, and she will bring them home.

In the afternoon, she plans to visit the old railroad warehouse the city government helpfully donated to her order. All she had to do was ask. When she greets the lepers who now reside there, she will touch each of them intentionally. Tenderly. So that they feel her love. So that they feel and know the love of Christ.

Later in the evening she will be swept away to the local airport to begin a long and arduous journey westward. She accepted an invitation to visit one of the order's orphanages in Paris. Or was it the home in the South Bronx, New York? She will need to find out. In any case, all of that is for later. All of that is for the future, which is a mystery to all but God.

For now, in the quietness of this simple morning, she settles in once again to pray. The words come easily, as they should—she has spoken them every morning for more years than she can remember:

"Dear Jesus, help us to spread Your fragrance everywhere we go. Flood our souls with Your Spirit and Life. Penetrate and possess our whole being so utterly that our lives may only be a radiance of Yours. Shine through us and be so in us that every soul we come in contact with may feel Your presence in our souls. Let them look up and see no longer us, but only Jesus!

"Stay with us and then we shall begin to shine as You shine, so as to be a light to others. The light, O Jesus, will be all from You; none of it will be ours. It will be You, shining on others through us.

"Let us thus praise You in the way You love best, by shining on those around us. Let us preach You without preaching, not by words but by example, by the catching force, the sympathetic influence of what we do, the evident fullness of the love our hearts bear for You. Amen."[1]

Have you guessed the identity of this mystery woman? Her given name was Anjezë Gonxhe Bojaxhiu, but the world knows her best by a different title.

You know her as Mother Teresa.

At the age of eighteen, Mother Teresa began a life of

missionary service—a ministry she lived and breathed for seventy years. In that time, she sought out "the unwanted, the unloved, the uncared for" among the streets and slums of Calcutta. She founded her own order, the Missionaries of Charity, within the Catholic Church—an order that has since expanded to include thousands of members in more than 140 countries. She launched orphanages and schools, hospitals and food banks. She helped care for orphans, lepers, the diseased, and the dying. She was among the first to establish a clinic for HIV/AIDS victims in the 1980s. And in her many public appearances, she was a regular and stalwart supporter of the truths recorded in God's Word.[2]

Mother Teresa lived as a shining example of Jesus' command to bless "the least of these." Yet her many accomplishments were not based on her own goodness or her own strength, though both were considerable. Instead, she founded her ministry on the rock of God's goodness and God's strength—a practice that included daily setting herself before His throne by reciting the prayer offered above.

In short, the woman now revered as Saint Teresa of Calcutta is a testament to what can happen within a community and around the world when a woman prays.

Our Foundation for Life

Both today and throughout history, prayer has been a vital foundation for human culture and society.

The forms for that foundation were set when God first walked with Adam and Eve in the cool of the garden. From the beginning, humanity was hardwired to live in communication with our Creator. Then, the concrete for that foundation was poured over the course of centuries as God called out a people through which He revealed Himself to the world.

Abraham was a man of faith who lived in constant communication with God; as a result, God promised to bless his descendants by making them a great nation, and that through Abraham "all peoples on earth will be blessed" (Gen. 12:3). Jacob's name was changed to Israel—"he struggles with God"—when he spent a night wrestling with God, which is a picture of prayer. Moses, perhaps the greatest leader the world has ever seen, was so dedicated to prayer that he regularly met with God "face to face, as one speaks to a friend" (Ex. 33:11). David, a man after God's own heart, wrote psalms and prayers to God with such poignancy that we still recite them thousands of years later.

God solidified the place of prayer as a foundation for our lives through the living example of Jesus Christ, who is God in the flesh. Our Lord made it a daily custom to go out "very early in the morning, while it was still dark," to pray (Mark 1:35). Later, Jesus taught the world how to pray when He said, "Our Father in heaven, hallowed be your name" (Matt. 6:9). And on the night before the cross—the most important moment in human history—the Son bowed before the Father and prayed with such intensity that His sweat was like drops of blood. "Not my will, but yours be done" (Luke 22:42).

The New Testament writers took great pains to emphasize the critical role that prayer must play in our lives—as well as the benefits we receive by doing so. The apostle Paul wrote, "Do not be anxious about anything, but in every situation, by prayer and petition, with thanksgiving, present your requests to God" (Phil. 4:6). The result? We will find "the peace of God" (v. 7). James exhorted Christ's followers to "confess your sins to each other and pray for each other." Why? "So that you may be healed" (James 5:16). And the author of Hebrews encouraged us to "approach God's throne of grace with confidence, so that we may receive mercy and find grace to help us in our time of need" (Heb. 4:16).

Note that none of these scriptures are given as suggestions for us to consider. They are commands for us to obey.

It's worth repeating: both today and throughout history, prayer has been a vital foundation for all who choose to follow God. Indeed, without establishing a direct connection to God through prayer, we cannot follow Him. We will have no idea where He is leading.

Now, I may know what you're thinking as you've read through these pages. *Bishop Jakes, this is supposed to be a book about women praying, but you keep talking about men. You've got Abraham and Moses, David and Paul. What gives?*

My answer is that while there have been many great men of prayer as individuals over the course of millennia, it is women in general who have carried the lion's share of that load.

Both today and throughout history, women have been especially powerful in taking up the mantle of prayer. While men of old cut timbers and tilled the ground to build our homesteads and cities, it was largely the prayers of women that established the spiritual sanctuary of our families. As men took up arms to fight the great wars of history, the prayers and petitions of women have regularly stemmed the tide of evil in spiritual battle. And though the majority of leadership positions in our churches are filled by men, it is mostly women who fill our sanctuaries with prayers and shouts of praise that reach the very throne of God.

I have seen these truths played out in my own life. Both of my grandmothers were dedicated to prayer. They were fierce and determined women who took seriously their role as part of the spiritual bedrock in their families and their communities. My mother was busy as an educator and a real-estate investor, yet she willingly gave of herself each day to teach her children how to pray and to invest in our spiritual lives. And what can I say of my wife, Serita? She is my true partner in ministry and in life, yet I am frequently in awe of the ease with which she steps into God's presence and the power of her prayers.

I especially love the way Serita has prayed for our children throughout their lives. I can remember her holding each little baby in her arms, her head bowed and voice softly whispering blessings by each infant's sleeping ears. I can see her standing outside each child's room at night, her voice still quiet but her arms now raised in intercession. A warrior engaged in battle.

Even now I feel my heart stir at these memories. There is nothing like a mother's prayers!

Not only have I seen in my own life the wonder and the humility of women who pray, but I have also benefitted from such women—and benefitted greatly. I have no doubt I am writing these pages today because of the prayers of the matriarchs who came before me. Whatever success I have experienced in life and ministry has a direct connection to the women who have supported and encouraged me not only through their hard work and sound advice, but also through their constant prayers.

Our world is a stressful place in many ways. Life is constantly changing and continually presents new challenges. Yet I look to the future with confidence and joy. Why? Because I serve a great and mighty God. And because I have witnessed with my own eyes all the good that can happen when women pray.

A New Call to Prayer

Speaking of change, it's worth pointing out that changes in our world often bring about new blessings in our lives. That has been especially true for women in recent history.

As I look out across cultures and societies today, I see women breaking new ground and blazing new trails in every way imaginable. Women are climbing corporate ladders at rapid speeds and ascending to the highest levels of success. They are running countries, leading with integrity and passion. They are launching businesses and spearheading innovations. They are excelling in the classroom, in the boardroom, and in every room.

Amazingly, women have championed these advances outside the home without sacrificing the precious lives within their homes. Because of changes in both technology and social norms, modern women are balancing work and family in ways that would have seemed impossible to mothers of previous generations. They are marrying wonderful men of God and partnering to raise gifted children who in their turn will bless the world anew.

As a pastor, I'm gratified by the progress I have seen in the lives of women in my community and in the larger world. We all benefit from these advances. We all win when women influence society to a greater degree.

As a father, however—and especially a father of daughters—it's difficult to express the depth of my gratitude. What a joy and a blessing to know that the women of earlier generations have opened new doors for my daughters, and that my daughters now have the opportunity to carve out exciting new vistas for their children.

Praise God!

Still, there's a danger that in our march toward progress and prosperity we may leave behind one of the key ingredients to our success. I am speaking about prayer.

This book is a call for women of all generations to continue their march toward equality and empowerment, yet to do so by once again embracing the power of prayer. This is a call for women in every community to dream like their daughters and pray like their grandmothers.

The world of the future will need women who understand both the power and the protection available only through prayer. We will need women warriors who can raise their swords in the continuing fight against oppression and injustice, and we will need women with shields to defend the innocent and the untrained.

It is only through prayer that such a widespread movement will be sustained. It is only through prayer that these wonderful advances will not only hold but continue forward.

Just as important, I want women to remember the wonder of prayer not only as a general principle but as something vital in their own lives. Prayer is a stress reliever. It's a chain breaker. It's a peace bringer, and it's necessary for every child of God, no matter their age or experience.

I remember watching a conversation between Oprah Winfrey and Maya Angelou on *SuperSoul Sunday*. Talking about prayer, Angelou said, "It changes things." How true that is!

Angelou went on to describe the ways she has personally benefited from prayer. "I know that when I pray, something wonderful happens. Not just to the person or persons for whom I'm praying, but also something wonderful happens to me. I'm grateful that I'm heard."[3]

That's what I want for you. To be heard. To be sustained. To find the joy and the peace and the confidence your Creator intended you to receive from Him long before the foundations of the earth were set down.

In the pages that follow, you will find stories of women who lived out these truths. Specifically, you will find ten women of the Bible whose propensity to pray in all circumstances set them apart as shining examples in the darkness of the ancient world.

As you read, I pray the light reflected by these women will both illuminate your mind and inspire your heart to follow in their example. I pray you will know the depth of insight, the breadth of compassion, and the height of worship all women can experience when they actively and intentionally bend their knees to pray.

CHAPTER I

Hannah

When women pray, God brings about new life.

It had been a long day, and Eli settled gratefully into his chair near the doorway of the tabernacle. He stretched his legs and flexed his toes, working out the aches and pains long familiar from years of work.

Around him, the city of Shiloh buzzed with activity. A large group of travelers had arrived to offer their sacrifices to God. People and cattle milled about the various courts and lawns, each waiting for their turn. The smell of fire and smoke was strong in the air, infused with the tantalizing aroma of roasted meat.

From his chair, Eli could hear the voices of his sons,

Hophni and Phinehas, as they performed the sacrifices within the interior of the tabernacle. Proclamations of blessing over families and children. Declarations of forgiveness. Vows and exhortations offered to God along with the necessary meat and salt and bread.

Because of his advanced age, Eli had passed much of the responsibility for these sacrifices down to his sons. But he remained the high priest, which meant there was still much for him to do. Much to accomplish and many people to greet. But for now he lingered in his chair, savoring the rest.

A motion at the corner of his eye caused Eli to glance out across the lawn. He saw a woman walking alone, which was unusual. No, not really walking—more like staggering. She had hugged both of her arms across her chest and was lurching and bouncing between people and horses and cattle as if her eyes were closed. When she turned in his direction, Eli saw her eyes *were* closed. More than that, her lips were moving rapidly without making any sound. She was mumbling to herself.

The old priest shook his head. He had seen it many times before. Wealthy families who offered large sacrifices shared a large meal together with their portion of the meat—which they often supplemented with more-than-generous portions of wine.

What was meant to be a celebration of God's goodness and the cleansing of sin could quickly slide into debauchery.

"How long are you going to stay drunk?" Eli called out to the woman. He was a little surprised at his own outburst, but he hated to see such corruption so near to God's own house. "Put away your wine!"

When the woman opened her eyes and looked into his, Eli flinched. He couldn't help it. The pain he saw in her face told him he had been wrong in his judgment.

Oh, so wrong.

Two Truths about Hannah

Hannah, the woman described above, is the first woman of prayer I want to highlight in these pages. There are several reasons for that choice. For one thing, Hannah's story is fascinating. It's also poignant and inspirational. But the main reason I am beginning this book with Hannah is that her story is so approachable. It's relatable.

I can say with confidence that Hannah's story will connect with your story in many important ways.

As we begin, there are two truths we need to know

about Hannah in order to truly understand the depth of her story. The first is that Hannah lived with an unfulfilled longing.

In 1 Samuel we read that Hannah was married to a wealthy man named Elkanah. We know he was wealthy because he had enough resources to travel with his entire family to God's tabernacle at Shiloh every year in order to make sacrifices on behalf of his family. Not only that, the sacrifices Elkanah offered were cattle—sheep or goats or bulls. In the Jewish law, the poorer families of Israel were allowed to use bread or grain for their sacrifices, or perhaps a pair of birds. But Elkanah had a ready supply of meat. He was wealthy.

There's more. Not only was Hannah married to a wealthy man, the Scriptures say "he loved her" (1:5), meaning that she had been blessed with financial stability, a loving spouse, and spiritual vitality within her household.

What then could be wrong? What else could be missing?

The answer was children. Hannah was barren. Instead of carrying a child, she carried an unfulfilled longing. But there's another layer to Hannah's longing that is important to lay bare if we want to understand the depth of her situation—the depth of her sorrow.

Way back in the book of Genesis, God made a

promise to Eve that one of her descendants would rise up and crush the head of the serpent we know as Satan. The verse is Genesis 3:15, which theologians call the *protevangelium*—"first gospel." With the benefit of history, we know that prophecy refers to Jesus, whose death on the cross was the hammer blow that crushed Satan's plans and power for all eternity.

For the ancient Israelites, however, the promise of Genesis 3:15 was a constant source of hope. No matter how dark the world became, no matter how sinister people behaved, there remained a promise from the Creator that evil would be defeated. As a result, Hebrew women counted themselves blessed through childbearing. Every new life kindled in every womb was an extension of God's promise to one day make right all that had been made wrong.

Therefore, Hannah's longing was not only for a child, but for the chance to participate in that blessing. That promise. She wanted a chance to deliver the One who would ultimately deliver everyone. Her barrenness excluded her from that opportunity, which made her unfulfilled longing all the more painful.

My father taught me never to ask a question when I already know the answer, so I won't ask whether you, too, have an unfulfilled longing. I already know you do.

Maybe you are similar to Hannah in that you have longed for years to feel the soft skin of an infant against your cheek and hear the laughter of children in your home. Maybe you yearn for a spouse to share your life with, or maybe you wish your current spouse would touch you and speak to you with tenderness rather than sharpness. Maybe your longing is for a career that would help you find meaning and purpose. Maybe it's financial stability. Maybe it's a house in which you can feel safe. Maybe it's a deeper knowledge of God and deeper experiences with Him.

Whatever your specific desire may be, we all carry the burden of unfulfilled longings. We all feel the burden and the void of dreams yet to come true.

The second truth we need to know about Hannah is that she had a rival. The Scriptures say Elkanah had two wives: Hannah and Peninnah. And listen to this: "Peninnah had children, but Hannah had none" (1 Sam. 1:2).

Can you feel the pain in that verse? The frustration? The text goes on to say that Peninnah continually "provoked" Hannah about their situation. She would intentionally push Hannah's buttons and remind her of her barrenness. This happened so frequently and so painfully that Hannah often "wept and would not eat" (1:7). She constantly mourned her lack of children, and she was constantly reminded of that lack because of her rival.

From Provocation to Prayer

How do you respond when you feel provoked? I'm not asking how people are *supposed* to respond or how you would *like* to respond. How *do* you respond?

As an example, how do you respond when someone who looks the way you would like to look first comes into your orbit? Or your husband's orbit? How do you respond when a coworker lands the promotion you deserve? How do you respond when that mother at the park says something nasty because your kids aren't behaving as well as hers? How do you respond when you are provoked by a rival?

In my experience, there are two basic choices we can make when we respond to provocation. The first choice is to get jealous. To become envious.

When you see someone living out a blessing you have longed to receive, you get that bitter taste in your mouth. You covet, imagining how sweet life would be if you had what she has and she were stuck with what you've been dealing with all these years. *She doesn't even appreciate what she's got. Why in the world would*

God be so generous in her life when I've been praying and sacrificing and working for so much longer than she has?

You can even reach a point in your envy and your bitterness that you try to tear the other person down to make yourself feel better. You can fool yourself into believing that making your rival feel smaller will somehow increase your own stature.

Or, you might even get cynical toward God Himself. *Lord, You know I deserve this blessing more than she does. God, I cannot believe You have ignored me month after month, year after year, and yet You respond instantly to the needs of someone who doesn't even worship You. It's not fair!*

Speaking frankly, the temptation to walk this path is strong for pastors and preachers. I remember many times during the early decades of my ministry when I would look around at others and feel the pull toward envy. Toward bitterness. *Imagine the impact I could make if I had that kind of platform. Imagine what our church could accomplish if we had this church's budget or that church's building.* Many times I was in danger of drifting into cynicism but for the wise counsel of those God had placed in my life to guide me toward a better way.

Thankfully, there is a better way.

The second choice you can make when you are provoked by a rival is to pray. Specifically, you can recognize that if God chose to birth a blessing in your rival's life, then He has the power to birth that same blessing—or an even greater blessing—in you. Which means you should turn to Him in prayer and ask for that blessing rather that lay hands on what has already been given to someone else.

Do you realize that God often *intentionally* brings rivals into your life to provoke you? Not to provoke you to anger or jealousy, but to provoke you toward greatness. To poke you and prod you toward the potential He sees in you. When you encounter those who look better, do better, have better, love better, wear better, drive better—whatever the "better" is—you need to understand there is a real possibility God is using that provocation to point you toward Himself so that He can bless you in the same way.

Hannah chose the path of prayer. After a particularly painful dinner confrontation with Peninnah while the family was in Shiloh, Hannah rose from the table and prayed her way to the tabernacle. God's house.

When Eli saw her, she was "in deep anguish" and "weeping bitterly." She appealed to the Lord: "If you will only look on your servant's misery and remember

me, and not forget your servant but give her a son"
(1:11). After the high priest confronted her, Hannah
answered by saying, "I have not been drinking wine
or beer; I was pouring out my soul to the Lord. Do
not take your servant for a wicked woman; I have
been praying here out of my great anguish and grief"
(1:15–16).

Let me stop the story for a moment and offer a
principle I believe is critical for prayer: whenever you
approach the throne of God, be yourself.

Notice that Hannah did not rely on flowery language or ten-dollar words as she prayed. She cried out
to God. Even as she wept bitterly, she wove an appeal
through her weeping. She prayed with intensity. She
prayed with fervency. She prayed with such passion
and such desire that Eli believed her to be drunk. May
the same be said of us! May the same be true of us
when we bow our faces to the ground in front of our
Heavenly Father and plead with Him about our deepest needs.

Do you sometimes feel God would grant your
request if only you knew the right words to pray? If
only you could find that exact turn of phrase? Reject
that thought. There are no magic words in prayer.
There is only the grace of God.

Do you sometimes believe your prayers would be answered if only someone special would pray for you? Someone anointed? Someone more spiritual than you or more holy than you? Reject that notion. The Bible says, "There is no one righteous, not even one" (Rom. 3:10). You don't need any person to make your prayers more effective. You need God's Holy Spirit to intercede on your behalf.

Do you assume God would pay more attention to your prayers if you were a better person? Or do you try to behave better or act more "godly" on the days you pray because you think God will take you more seriously when you are more spiritual? Stop it. You can't twist God's arm and make Him do what you want; you can only kneel at His feet, pour out your heart, and believe He will answer—and that His answer will be for your benefit.

In short, when you come before God in prayer, come as you are. Stop worrying about your image and stop worrying about what you look like or what people might think about you. Fall on your knees before God with passion and fervency, and He will open the windows of heaven and pour out a blessing you won't have room enough to receive!

That's what Hannah experienced.

Blessings of Life

I love what the Scripture says in 1 Samuel 1:19: "Early the next morning they arose and worshiped before the Lord and then went back to their home at Ramah. Elkanah made love to his wife Hannah, and the Lord remembered her."

It's the last phrase in verse 19 that gets me every time: "the Lord remembered her." Why? Because she prayed.

Now, that doesn't mean God had forgotten about Hannah prior to that prayer. This was not a situation where God was out washing the car in the driveway and received a heavenly text message that said, "Hannah wants a baby," then He smacked His forehead and said, "I forgot about her." No! Our God is all-knowing and all-seeing. He is sovereign at all times, and He is constantly aware of every single moment of our lives.

The word *remembered* in verse 19 is a way of signaling in the Hebrew language that God made a decision to act. God had heard every one of Hannah's past prayers throughout all the years of her life. He had answered every previous prayer by saying, "Wait." "Wait." "Not yet." "Still not yet."

But in this moment, after this specific prayer,

God remembered Hannah and changed His answer. Responding to that prayer, He said yes. As a result, "in the course of time Hannah became pregnant and gave birth to a son" (1:20).

Let me say something from the depths of my heart that I hope you will hear: God remembers you. I know you may find that difficult to believe, but hear me: He remembers you. He has always remembered you!

All the nights you wondered and worried about the future, God remembered you. All the times you did without, He remembered you. All the times you hugged a pillow and cried yourself to sleep, He saw you and stood by you and remembered you. Yes, sometimes you do things for other people and they forget you, but God doesn't forget you. I believe the Lord planned from the beginning of time for you to be right here in this moment reading the words on this page because He wants you to know He remembers you.

God has not forgotten you. Just as He did not forget Hannah.

More than that, God has a plan for you, just as He had a plan for Hannah. Specifically, He had a plan to bring a blessing to her body—to give life to her life.

God actively desires to create new life in our world. He actively desires to bring new life into your family.

Even when you believe your dream is dead, God is ready and willing to resurrect that dream and breathe life into what you thought was lost.

That's why I'm so excited to see a new generation of women who pray—because prayer is the key that unlocks God's blessings!

Look at what Hannah said in verse 20: "She named him Samuel, saying, 'Because I asked the Lord for him.'" She asked. That is the beauty and the simplicity of prayer. We often make prayer more complicated than it needs to be, but at the core prayer is simply talking with God. It's telling Him about our needs and desires and asking Him to act. It's also listening to His voice when He answers those requests—because He does answer.

The name *Samuel* means "heard by God." Isn't it wonderful to know that we serve a God who hears us? We don't serve the idols of old that were deaf and dumb because they were carved by human hands. We serve a God whose hands reach out to touch us, whose eyes watch us with tenderness, and whose ears are always attentive to our prayers.

Take a moment to think about your unfulfilled longings—those dreams and desires you've carried for what seems like a lifetime. Are you talking to God about them? Have you asked God to receive them?

If so, keep asking. He hears you. He has not forgotten you.

If you have not been asking God to receive those longings, there is no better time than the present. You don't need fancy words. You don't need to clean yourself up or find a preacher to pray on your behalf. Simply come to God as you are—and ask.

Because when women pray, God brings about new life.

CHAPTER 2

Mary

*When women pray, God brings redemption and
reconciliation into darkness.*

The young woman sat on the dirt in front of her
family home, arms wrapped protectively around
her knees and head down. Shaking slightly from silent
sobs, she felt more like the girl she used to be than the
woman everyone expected her to become.

Just a few years ago, she'd been content to live as a
child. Carefree. When she hadn't been required to help
her mother with meals and housework, she'd been
able to run with the other children through the streets
of Nazareth and out into the open spaces. They used

to throw stones off the cliffs and listen as they clattered down the rocky slopes.

Now, everything was different.

Even a few months ago, life had been normal. Better than normal—it had been sweet. Abundant. Joseph had chosen her. Proposed to her. They had walked those same streets together, talking and dreaming about everything the future would hold. He was a good man. A carpenter, proud of what he could build. He had a good family, with roots all the way back to King David himself.

Now, everything had changed.

Joseph had been gentle when they last talked. Even kind. But he'd also been firm. He said he wouldn't shame her publicly. The divorce would be quiet. As respectable as possible. But their betrothal was finished. There would be no future. No more dreams. No house built with his own hands—at least, not for her.

Mary held her breath for a few moments, then let it out. A sigh of frustration and pain. For the thousandth time, she thought back to the morning when everything became so complicated.

The angel said I was highly favored, she thought. *He said the Lord is with me. But is it true? How could it be true?*

Mary's hand drifted unconsciously to her belly,

resting on the gentle swell of new life that had recently begun to show. That part of the angel's message had certainly been true. She had never been with a man, and yet she was with child. And no matter how quiet Joseph was while securing the divorce, pretty soon everybody in Nazareth would know.

She bowed her head again, this time to pray. *My God, how do I move forward? How will I survive this?*

Is there any way I can convince him to stay?

It's Complicated

There have been many times in my life when I have wished I could escape from the spotlight. Just drift into obscurity for a few weeks. Even long before I became a speaker and author with an audience and all that, there were plenty of moments I wished I could escape the spotlight of my community. Or my friends. Or my family.

Sometimes it's much more comfortable to be unknown and unseen.

As I have spoken with women around the globe in recent years, it has become increasingly clear that the spotlight is wider and more penetrating than ever before. We live in a world and a season in history where everyone is watching everyone. Because of technology and social media, it seems as if everyone has access to everyone, which means everyone is constantly aware of the spotlight.

Not only that, but we live in a world and in a season where there is unprecedented pressure to pretend that life is easy. That we've got everything figured out and everything under control. That we are healthy, wealthy, wise, happy, and free, with no storm clouds on the horizon.

Mary understood the truth. She knew life is complicated.

We also understand that life is complicated. We know it from experience—although we often feel pressured to pretend otherwise. Maybe that's true of you.

When you have your small group over to dinner on Thursday night, the house is spotless. The windows and mirrors sparkle in the light. Not a speck of dust in the air or on the blinds. Your guests can still see the fresh lines in the carpet left by your vacuum cleaner, and there is no sign of clutter in any corner. A place for everything and everything in its place. But if those same guests had shown up unexpectedly on Monday night, what would they have found? What about Wednesday morning? What about Thursday an hour before the small group was scheduled to start?

It's complicated.

Mary

When you show up to work on Monday, you are confident, clear, and in control. First of all, you look great. You've got a plan put together for the whole week—every project you intend to tackle and achieve, and everything you will assign to your employees. It's even color coded. You are the very picture of a model manager ready to lead your team to victory. But if that team could see past the façade of your external reality, what would they find inside? What if they could see your fear? Your doubt? Your stress? Your frustration? What would they think?

It's complicated.

When your neighbors walk by your home each morning, they can't help but feel a stab of envy. They've seen the car you drive. They watched as the new porch was constructed out back (although you call it a pergola). They've seen the way your children mow the yard and pick the weeds every Saturday morning. They even saw you and your husband kissing on the porch after your Friday date night. But what if those same neighbors could see inside the walls? What if they could see your credit card bill? What if they could hear the arguments? What if they could feel what you feel when dinnertime has come and gone and your husband forgot to call—again. How would you feel if they knew everything you know?

It's complicated.

As I say, Mary knew the truth about life because her life had become complicated. Look at what the scripture says: "This is how the birth of Jesus the Messiah came about: His mother Mary was pledged to be married to Joseph, but before they came together, she was found to be pregnant through the Holy Spirit. Because Joseph her husband was faithful to the law, and yet did not want to expose her to public disgrace, he had in mind to divorce her quietly" (Matt. 1:18–19).

Imagine how confusing it must have been for Mary when it all started going wrong. Her fiancé decided to end their relationship. She was a pregnant teenager in a society where pregnant teenagers could legally be stoned to death. At best, she was looking down the barrel of a lifetime of rejection and ridicule from a close-knit community she could not escape.

What must have been especially confusing—especially painful—is that Mary's circumstances seemed to directly contradict the promises she had received from God.

Highly Favored

If I ask someone today how they are feeling or how their day is going, I'm likely to get a one-word answer:

"Fine." That's how we respond to questions about ourselves today. "I'm fine." Things were different back when I was growing up. Back then, if I asked some of the elders in our church how they were doing, they would always say the same thing: "I am blessed and highly favored."

That's the first promise Mary received from the angel Gabriel when he appeared to tell her what was about to happen in her life. "The angel went to her and said, 'Greetings, you who are highly favored! The Lord is with you'" (Luke 1:28).

Do you see the second promise? "The Lord is with you." I don't have to tell you that both of those promises are good news. But I also don't have to tell you that Mary had a difficult time understanding how those promises connected with the reality of her life once the consequences of her pregnancy began to bloom.

What does it mean, then, to be highly favored? Theologically, it means to be highly graced. It doesn't mean you're better than other people. It doesn't mean you will suddenly avoid or rise above all the problems in your life. It means you have been touched by God's grace, as Mary was.

Let me say something you may need to hear, even if you find it difficult to believe: you are highly favored.

If you are hanging strong in your marriage even though there are difficulties, you are highly favored. If you have children in the home or out of the home who are making good choices and reaching upward to better themselves and be productive in society, you are highly favored. If you are holding down a job that helps put food on your table and pay the bills each month, you are highly favored. If you've got a college degree, you are highly favored. If you have a spouse you can lean on or a friend you can confide in or a bathtub you can hide in for a few moments of peace each day, you are highly favored.

In short, if you have received any kind of blessing and provision in your life, then you are highly favored. Why? Because you did nothing to earn or deserve those blessings. You are a recipient of God's grace.

There's another aspect that's worth exploring regarding Mary's angelic message. Namely, she did not know she was highly favored before the angel spoke those words to her heart and soul. She did not know the Lord was with her. But she needed to know.

Think about it: you don't need a messenger to explain something you already understand. God is not wasteful of His messengers or of our time. He would never send a messenger to tell me that I'm a man. He would never send a messenger to teach me what it means to be African American—I already know from experience.

In short, God does not speak into our lives to tell us what we already know. He speaks into our lives to tell us what we need to hear. Just as He did with Mary.

Consider all the trials Mary endured from the moment of Jesus' conception to the moment of His crucifixion. There were blessings, yes, but think of all the trouble. Think of all the pain. I've already mentioned the danger and the shame of being pregnant and unmarried in a judgmental society. But think of the discomfort she experienced while riding from Nazareth to Bethlehem on the back of a donkey—a journey of about ninety miles. Think of the humiliation she experienced giving birth in the back of a barn, not to mention the pain and the lack of medical care. Think of the terror she endured fleeing with her family in the middle of the night to escape a crazed and murderous king. Think of this young and inexperienced girl surviving exile in Egypt for two years while assassins tracked her every move.

In all that hardship, Mary needed to know that she was highly favored. She needed to know God was with her. That knowledge may have been the only thing that kept her going.

Eventually, Mary came to understand the truth of her favor with God. We know this because Scripture records one of her prayers during the turbulent period of her pregnancy. Here's how that prayer began:

> My soul glorifies the Lord
> and my spirit rejoices in God my Savior,
> for he has been mindful
> of the humble state of his servant.
> From now on all generations will call me
> blessed,
> for the Mighty One has done great things
> for me—
> holy is his name. (Luke 1:46–49)

Mary responded to God's grace in her life by declaring a prayer of praise. She did not glorify God merely with her lips, but all the way down to her soul. She praised the Lord from her innermost being because she understood she had been blessed.

May the same be true of you and me. Because we are highly favored.

Darkness and Light

If you continue to read Mary's prayer as recorded in Luke 1, you will find a powerful prophecy about many of the wonderful things that would be accomplished through the child God had kindled in Mary's womb. That child, of course, was Jesus, whom we know as the Christ. The Messiah. The Mighty One. God in flesh.

In her prayer, Mary prophesied that Jesus would extend God's mercy to the people. And not just the people of her day, but from generation to generation. Mary prophesied that Jesus would perform mighty deeds and scatter those whose hearts are filled with pride. She prophesied that Jesus would cast down rulers from their thrones and lift up the humble. She prophesied that Jesus would feed the hungry and rebuke the rich. And she prophesied that Jesus would fulfill the promises made long ago to His servant Abraham—specifically the promise to bless "all peoples on earth" (Gen. 12:3).

In other words, Mary prophesied that Jesus would bring light into the darkness of the world. And not just *her* world, but ours as well.

The apostle John affirmed this mission in Jesus' life when he wrote,

> In the beginning was the Word, and the Word was with God, and the Word was God. He was with God in the beginning. Through him all things were made; without

him nothing was made that has been made. In him was life, and that life was the light of all mankind. The light shines in the darkness, and the darkness has not overcome it. (John 1:1–5)

Jesus Himself affirmed this mission when He said, "I am the light of the world. Whoever follows me will never walk in darkness, but will have the light of life" (John 8:12).

So let me ask you: what are some ways you have experienced the darkness of this world? Notice I don't ask *if* you've experienced darkness, because I know you have. Each of us confronts that darkness in different ways, but none of us is immune. How are you experiencing darkness right now? Right this very moment?

Whatever your circumstances may be, let me encourage you to pray for light.

That is a principle I hope you will highlight here on this page or write down somewhere, because it's worth remembering: when you are surrounded by a darkness that threatens to overwhelm your very soul, your only hope is prayer.

Your only source of relief is to remember that darkness is never stronger than light. And you have access to *the* Light when you turn to Him in prayer.

This Present Darkness

I am writing these words during a heavy period of darkness. Specifically, I am writing while the world is in the grip of a pandemic known as COVID-19. I'm writing from my home rather than my usual office because the Dallas metro area, where I live, has been locked down in a state of semi-quarantine for more than a month.

Because of the virus, people have been discouraged from leaving their houses. People have been ordered not to report to work except for specific essential functions. Churches have been closed down. Schools are no longer in session. Our local supermarkets are in danger of becoming empty while our hospitals are in danger of becoming full.

This is a time of fear unlike any I have seen in years—a time where many are feeling the pull toward panic. And this is true not just in Dallas, not just in Texas, not just in the United States, but around the entire world.

As a pastor, I feel the heaviness of this present darkness because it has impacted my relationship with my church. I count it a privilege of extreme value to stand before my congregation each Sunday and lead them into the glorious presence of God. There are faces I see every week to encourage me and inspire me. Our choir is one of the most talented I have ever encountered, and I relish each moment I stand in their presence as they lead our entire congregation to the throne of God.

Yet for weeks now, I have been denied those privileges. Those blessings. Yes, our church has adapted; our staff is doing everything possible to create an online experience that is beneficial for anyone who joins us. But it's not the same.

Plainly and simply, I miss my community. I miss my church.

I also feel the heaviness of this present darkness because it has exposed our vulnerability as a species more effectively and more efficiently than anything in recent memory. In my own country of America, many have lived for years in the false belief that they were above the terrors of life experienced by other nations around the world—terrors of disease and corruption and ineffectiveness and mass panic. Americans often feel their resources and their technology and their riches relative to the rest of the world will insulate them against pandemics and other struggles.

COVID-19 has proven the falsity of such beliefs. In many ways, this pandemic has served as a great equalizer in our societies. It has pressed down on the rich and poor alike. It has forced both millennials and baby boomers to shelter in place. It hampers Republicans, Democrats, Libertarians, anarchists, and all other political affiliations. It has even broken down the silos of fame and fortune, reaching into the lives of celebrities as well as common folk.

In another sense, however, COVID-19 has shown a spotlight on the injustices that have existed in our societies for centuries. African Americans make up 14 percent of the total population in America, yet they represent at least 33 percent of COVID-19 deaths.[1] Many are quick to point out that the virus targets those with preexisting conditions, such as heart disease, diabetes, and obesity. What the pundits often forget, however, is that many of those preexisting conditions are consequences of injustice rather than the result of personal choice.

People don't choose to live in poverty, but those who do live in poverty are typically unhealthy. They lack the resources to afford regular health care or expensive gym memberships. Often they lack access to the best doctors because of the ways our society is segregated. Many times they lack education on the best choices for a healthy lifestyle, including diet and nutrition.

In a similar way, how do you practice social distancing when you have eight people living in a two-bedroom house? How do you work from home when you've got two or three jobs? How do you provide for your family when both you and your spouse work in the service industry—which is common for people of color—and the service industry has closed its doors in your face?

None of these issues were caused by COVID-19. Instead, the pandemic has laid bare that which has been hiding in plain sight. When I hear about those statistics, I wonder how many of those people of color who passed away are my people? How many are readers of my books? How many have attended our conferences and gatherings?

If I make speak personally once again, part of me is apprehensive about what I'll experience when we are finally able to open our church doors once more. How many people will I miss that first Sunday? How many hands that I have shaken are currently reaching out in isolated hospital rooms with no one to take hold of? How many mouths that sang along with me week after week in years past are now hooked up to ventilators? How many faces that I have watched and known among my congregation are even now cooling in makeshift morgues, their voices lost and their eyes closed forever?

Perhaps the most disturbing consequence of COVID-19 for many in my culture is the loss of funerals. If that sounds strange to you, understand that funerals are a big deal in the black community here in America and in many other communities across the globe. For many people, their funeral is the one place where they get to be important. It's the place where everyone gathers to recognize not that they died, but that they lived—that their life mattered. To be denied even that dignity by an unseen virus is especially horrifying.

These are haunting thoughts. These are serious times. This is a manifestation of darkness that has shaken many to the core, myself included.

Yet I am not afraid. Not because I'm strong or because I have access to physical resources others are unable to acquire. Not because I have any direct line to health-care resources that are growing increasingly scarce.

No, I am unafraid because I have access to spiritual resources through prayer. I have access to Jesus, who brings light into the darkness. I have access to God, who, in Mary's words, is the "Mighty One" who can accomplish "great things for me."

I have that access through prayer, and so do you.

Not only that, but I remain unafraid in this current

crisis because I am surrounded by women who understand the power of prayer. My wife is by my side. My daughters talk with me and pray with me every day. The women of our congregation at the Potter's House are united in prayer for our community and our country. And there is a network tens of thousands strong from our Woman Thou Art Loosed events who are standing in God's presence and making intercession for the world before His throne.

The wonderful truth that we can hold on to even in the midst of a pandemic is that darkness is never stronger than light. I choose to tether myself to that truth, and I urge you to do the same.

Reconciliation and Redemption

Let's conclude this chapter by returning to the relationship between Joseph and Mary. Why? Because there are few burdens that feel quite so heavy as the burden of broken relationships.

Have you felt that burden in your life? It settles across your shoulders when the person who used to say "I love you" now says "I don't want to see you." The weight of it threatens to bring you to your knees when the same child who used to smile with delight every time you entered a room now doesn't even answer your phone calls—let alone think to dial your number. You feel it when friends turn their backs on you because they don't like something you said or something you failed to say. You feel it when going to work is a struggle because your boss never sees what you contribute or always finds a way to tear you down.

Yes, strained relationships are a terrible burden. And broken relationships threaten to break us.

But there is hope for reconciliation. Just look at what happened to Joseph after he decided to end his relationship with Mary:

> But after he had considered this, an angel of the Lord appeared to him in a dream and said, "Joseph son of David, do not be afraid to take Mary home as your wife, because what is conceived in her is from the Holy Spirit. She will give birth to a son, and you are to give him the name Jesus, because he will save his people from their sins."
>
> All this took place to fulfill what the Lord had said through the prophet: "The virgin will conceive and give birth to a son, and they will call him Immanuel" (which means "God with us").

When Joseph woke up, he did what the angel
of the Lord had commanded him and took
Mary home as his wife. (Matthew 1:20–24)

As a side note, in all the years of Joseph's life, how many times do you think he stopped to thank God in his prayers for sending this angel? I would venture it was in the thousands. Because Mary was a woman worth having. Mary was a catch. Mary was the kind of wife that men reference when they say they "outkicked their coverage."

Sometimes we allow Mary's virginity in this entire episode to overshadow the other admirable elements of her character. For example, one of the qualities I like most about Mary is her tenacity. Mary was a tenacious woman. In the face of all kinds of obstacles and all kinds of trials, she fought without surrender. And she fought not for herself but for the life of her child. For her family.

There has been an epidemic in the world over recent decades that encourages women to choose an easier path than Mary chose. There is a philosophy or a way of thinking that tells women to elevate themselves and their needs and their wants and their careers and their free time and their hobbies—to elevate everything they desire over their families and over their children.

I believe that is a tragedy. Not because women are not valuable, but because there is incredible value in offering ourselves for the ones we love most, as Mary did.

I praise Mary for the tenacity she showed in serving her family. And I sing the praises of every woman who chooses to keep her child even when the road ahead seems difficult. I praise every working mother who fights tenaciously to hold close to her children even as she holds down a job. I praise every wife who chooses to willingly set aside her own career in service to her family. And I praise every single mother who finds a way to work a career month after month and year after year, and still provide the nurture and the care her children need.

We need more tenacious women in this world. We need more women so fierce and fiery that their men thank God every day for whatever guardian angel brought them into their lives.

Now, back to Joseph's dream. I can hear someone out there say, "Bishop Jakes, God has never sent an angel to find me a man. And God has never sent an angel to make any of my problems just disappear. How does this story apply to my situation in a modern world?"

First of all, who says God has never sent an angel to help solve your problems? Angels are spirit beings, but they impact our world all the time. Certainly God has used angels to help you in your struggles against the darkness.

More important, let me ask a question in return: *Why* did God send this angel to speak into Joseph's dreams? What caused it?

I believe the answer is that Mary prayed. We've already seen how Mary lifted up her voice in praise to God even in the midst of a difficult situation. It's reasonable, then, to expect that Mary approached God with her needs and desires—specifically her desire for reconciliation between herself and Joseph.

Here's another principle: when you see no hope for reconciliation in your broken relationships, your best hope is to pray, because God is capable of making momentous things happen in order to restore what has been lost.

Not only did God accomplish reconciliation between Joseph and Mary, but Mary's prayers resulted in reconciliation between God and humanity. That's because the final result of Mary's prayers was the birth, life, death, and resurrection of Jesus Christ. Mary's faithfulness to pray—and to respond to what God communicated to her in prayer—resulted in the incredible gift of eternal life offered to all who would receive it.

This is what we commonly refer to as salvation,

although there's another term Scripture often uses to describe it: *redemption*. Interestingly, redemption is a financial concept. It means "to buy out." Originally, it was a term used when someone purchased the debt incurred by a slave—to redeem a slave meant to buy their freedom.

That is what Jesus has done for us. He has redeemed us. He canceled the debt of our slavery to sin and purchased our freedom at the cost of His own life. Paul wrote that in Jesus, and in Jesus alone, "we have redemption through his blood, the forgiveness of sins, in accordance with the riches of God's grace" (Eph. 1:7).

Have you tasted that freedom? Do you want more life in your life? Do you want more light in your darkness? Do you want to see relationships healed and the very armies of heaven sent down to work on your behalf?

Then pray. Because when women pray, God brings reconciliation and redemption into the darkness of this world.

CHAPTER 3

Sarah

When women pray, they find hope and joy in unexpected places.

Everyone in the camp noticed when the old woman emerged from her tent. Sarah. The mistress.

Conversations ceased. Men who had been lounging in various shady spots quickly picked up whatever tools were nearby and returned to their work. Women adjusted their posture as they carried water or grain to and from the storehouses. Children, suddenly silent, instinctively faded into the background.

Sarah hid a smile as she stepped fully into the heat of the sun. She knew her reputation. It had been well earned for decades now. *Was I not rightly named Sarai as a child?*

She did not walk like an eighty-nine-year-old as she made her way toward the storehouses for her daily inspection. Her back was still straight, her steps still graceful. Her eyes still flashed and her mind—not to mention her tongue—remained sharp. But her thoughts were heavy.

How odd to be near the end, she thought. *How strange to feel this strong and yet feel certain that death is near.*

Sarah's life was full and had been full from the beginning. Born among the Chaldeans in Ur, she had been swept off her feet by Abraham and carried to a distant land. Adventure and comfort in the same package. Romance and mystery. There had been danger, too. Twice she had been taken into the harems of foreign kings—well, perhaps "given" was the more accurate word—and twice she had been rescued untouched through the hand of God.

I have wealth, servants, land, and power, she mused. *I have a loving husband and memories to treasure. I am blessed beyond all others I know.*

And yet…

A frown touched Sarah's lips as she watched a group of children tumbling together on the outskirts of the camp. The children of servants. The children of soldiers. The children of farmers and shepherds. And there was Ishmael, too, rolling on his back and kicking like a donkey. The only child of her husband. *But not my child.*

All her life, Sarah had watched other women raise their children. Sometimes she felt buried by the children of others.

She turned away from the sight. A rare retreat. She tried to push the image out of her mind. *I am an old woman even if I don't look like one,* she reminded herself. *I have sweated and shivered through my season of change. I am as dry and withered as the weeds growing out of this sand.*

And yet...

On days like these, Sarah had trouble pushing away the promises from her past. Promises spoken from God to Abraham: "I will make you into a great nation, and I will bless you." "A son who is your own flesh and blood will be your heir." "Your wife Sarah will bear you a son, and you will call him Isaac."

The promises were absurd. Impossible. Unthinkable given her own age, let alone Abraham's.

And yet... great God of heaven—the God of Abraham, my husband—could it still be true?

Secret Whispers

Sharp-eyed readers of Scripture may be curious about Sarah's inclusion in this book. After all, there are no prayers uttered by Sarah recorded in the pages of God's Word.

In answer, I would point those readers to Hebrews 11 in the New Testament, which theologians refer to as the "Hall of Faith." In this inspiring chapter, the author of Hebrews highlights women and men from the Old Testament who demonstrated an exceptional level of faith in God's power and promises.

Hebrews 11 is filled with the heroes of our faith, including Sarah: "And by faith even Sarah, who was past childbearing age, was enabled to bear children because she considered him faithful who had made the promise" (v. 11).

I would submit that it is impossible to demonstrate faith in God without knowing God. It is impossible to know God without communicating with God. And it is impossible to communicate with God without prayer. Therefore, I can state clearly and confidently that Sarah was a woman of prayer.

There's another reason I have included Sarah in these pages: I want you to understand that God is not bound by our ability to verbalize what we need or what we desire. By that I mean God is not restricted by our recitations. God is not limited by our larynxes. And God is not vexed without our voices.

In short, God's ability to act is not dependent on our ability to pray.

Yes, in many circumstances God prefers to wait for His people to pray before He unleashes His power in their lives. In many circumstances—perhaps even in most circumstances—God desires us to kneel before Him and pour ourselves out to Him in the spiritual form of communication we typically think of when we think of prayer. As C. S. Lewis wrote, "I've a sort of an idea he likes to be asked."[1]

But not in every circumstance.

Sometimes God hears the secret whispers of our hearts even when those whispers never escape our lips. Remember that God is omniscient—He knows all things, up to and including the thoughts in our minds and the longings in our hearts. And there are times God chooses to act based on those thoughts or longings without any official request from us.

Writing in the book of Romans, the apostle Paul described those who hope for what they need without fully understanding what is required to meet their needs. He wrote, "In the same way, the Spirit helps us in our weakness. We do not know what we ought to pray for, but the Spirit himself intercedes for us through wordless groans" (8:26).

Aren't you grateful that's true? Aren't you grateful God knows you better than you know yourself? Aren't you grateful that God's Spirit living inside you understands exactly what you need even when you are unable to articulate that need in a way that makes sense?

When you fooled yourself into believing you were in a healthy relationship with someone who genuinely cared about you, aren't you grateful God could see the secret pain inside your heart? Aren't you grateful He chose to save you from a lifetime of loneliness when you were desperate for companionship and ready to settle, even though you didn't know enough to ask Him?

When you resigned yourself to a mundane job, working the same schedule and pushing the same buttons week after week, month after month, year after year—aren't you grateful God heard your secret cry for significance? Aren't you grateful God knew that promotion was perfect for you and chose to bring it to you even when you didn't ask Him to make it happen?

When your spiritual life flagged and you lost all motivation to pursue a deeper connection and a deeper sense of intimacy with God—aren't you glad God saw you were drowning and stepped in to save you? Aren't you glad His Spirit swelled up inside you to convict you of your wrongdoing and your need to repent even though you were too wrapped up in yourself to pray?

I am grateful God hears the secret whispers, the secret longings in our lives. I'm grateful His Spirit maintains and monitors the deepest levels of our hearts. And I'm grateful He offers what we never knew we needed, just as He did for Sarah.

Unfortunately, it took Sarah a little time to accept what had been promised.

Laughing at God

How do you respond when you encounter God's promises? That's a critical question, because we all intersect with God's promises at various times in our lives.

Each of us receives specific promises from God that are unique to us as individuals. These are promises spoken directly to our spirits—truths we hear and incorporate into our lives without really understanding how or why they arrived. They are God-given guarantees of what He will accomplish if we choose to believe them and choose to respond in faith.

In addition, Scripture is filled with many general

promises of God. These are universal promises—they apply to all who have received salvation through faith in Jesus Christ.

For example, did you know there are dozens of times in the Bible where God promises strength to those who need it? Isaiah 40 says, "He gives strength to the weary and increases the power of the weak" (v. 29). The first book of Samuel says, "The bows of the warriors are broken, but those who stumbled are armed with strength" (2:4).

Or, what do you make of God's promise to give you wisdom whenever you ask for it? It's right there in black-and-white in the book of James: "If any of you lacks wisdom, you should ask God, who gives generously to all without finding fault, and it will be given to you" (1:5). This is not a suggestion. This is not a tip. This is not a hope or a wish or a dream. It's a promise. *It will be given to you.*

What about promises such as these?

1. "Therefore I tell you, whatever you ask for in prayer, believe that you have received it, and it will be yours" (Mark 11:24).
2. "My God will meet all your needs according to the riches of his glory in Christ Jesus" (Phil. 4:19).

3. "And we know that in all things God works for the good of those who love him, who have been called according to his purpose" (Rom. 8:28).

How do you handle these promises? What happens inside you when you read them?

Too often we respond to God's promises with cynicism. With unbelief. We take what God has offered and hold it up to the light with furrowed brows and squinting eyes, looking our God-given gift horse in the mouth. We bite the edge with our teeth like prospectors checking the authenticity of their gold. We waffle and waiver.

Maybe God does that kind of thing for other people, we think, *but not for me.*

I believe Sarah began her life with hope. With joy as well. In her youth, she cradled that hope against her chest the same way she planned to cradle her child. As the years passed, that hope became heavy. Harder to carry. Harder to pin against her skin and hang on to. Then, one sad and terrible day, she decided to let go.

Did you know hope can be aborted? Sarah did. And the pain of that loss was greater than anything she had experienced. She lost her hope and joy in the same moment.

It's not surprising, then, that Sarah was skeptical

when God opened the windows of heaven and declared she was about to have a son. In fact, she was more than skeptical. Abraham too. "Will a son be born to a man a hundred years old?" he said. "Will Sarah bear a child at the age of ninety?" (Gen. 17:17). When God told Abraham this promised son would arrive within a year, Sarah was listening in the background. Her only response was to laugh. To scoff. "After I am worn out and my lord is old, will I now have this pleasure?" (Gen. 18:12).

The question many readers want answered is, why? Why would Sarah laugh and settle for sarcasm when the greatest desire of her life had been set before her on a silver platter? Just a year away! God promised she would once more feel the pleasure of her husband's touch. God promised she would feel the stirring in her womb—the kicks and rolls of newly formed life. God promised her breasts would be filled with nourishment even as her heart would fill with joy.

It was everything she had been wanting and wishing for decades. Why couldn't she believe it? Why couldn't she accept it?

Perhaps a better question is, why can't we?

I believe Sarah's laughter was a defense mechanism. It was her way of protecting a heart suffering from the loss of hope. I believe the same is true of us today when we are confronted by promises that seem, for whatever reason, far too good to be true. After all, hope can be a painful thing when it stretches and strains without fulfillment; therefore, we resist the rekindling of that hope to avoid that pain. We build a wall of laughter against it, preferring the relative comfort of our status quo over the potential damage of disappointment renewed.

Thankfully, there's a better way. Yes, God's promises often seem too good to be true. But that's because God alone is able to provide that which is too good to be true! He is sovereign over all things, which means He can accomplish what we never dreamed possible.

Here is a principle: when you feel skeptical about a promise that seems too good to be true, your best hope is to pray. Seek God's will. If the promise is not from Him, He will confirm that through His Spirit inside you. If the promise does come from God, it's up to you to embrace it and watch what God can do when you respond to Him in faith.

Don't Settle

Sarah's past choices were another reason she laughed at God's promise—specifically, her choice to settle in the past for less than God's best. She tried to make her dreams come true through her own strength and her own ingenuity, and she failed.

That's how Ishmael came into the picture. When both Sarah and Abraham had reached middle age, Sarah panicked. She knew God had promised Abraham a son, yet that promise had not been delivered—nor did it look as if it would ever be delivered. As a result, Sarah took measures into her own hands: "The Lord has kept me from having children," she told Abraham. "Go, sleep with my slave; perhaps I can build a family through her" (Gen. 16:2).

I understand that waiting for God to fulfill His promises can be difficult. Like you, I have felt the weight of waiting. The burden. It piles up day after day, year after year until it begins to feel unbearable. Unmanageable.

But we can bear the weight when our waiting is matched with prayer. We can manage the years when our waiting is supported and uplifted by prayer—by a continued communication with the God who gave us the promise in the first place.

I am calling for a new generation of women who pray, because I am tired of watching people settle for less than God's best in their lives. I am tired of seeing church folk dragged down by waiting. I am tired of seeing God's people take matters into their own hands and build themselves counterfeit promises and counterfeit blessings.

This world needs women who will stand up and declare, for all to hear, "I will not settle! Even if I have to start over, I will not settle. Even if it takes longer than I ever imagined, I will not settle. Even if I have to make payments, I will not settle. Even if I have to raise these children on my own for a time, I will not settle. Even if I have to endure a boss who doesn't appreciate me, I will not settle. Even if I have to attend night school, I will not settle. Even if everyone I speak to about God's promises tells me I'm crazy and I am wasting my life, I will not settle."

No, you'll never make it on your own strength, but you don't have to. You can choose to pray and submit yourself to God's timing. You can trust Him to make good when it will produce the most good.

Yes, waiting for God's promises to come true is difficult work, but the payoff is worth it.

Sarah learned that truth—eventually. After twenty-five years of waiting, she received what God had promised. Scripture says, "Now the Lord was gracious to Sarah as he had said, and the Lord did for Sarah what he had promised. Sarah became pregnant and bore a son to Abraham in his old age, at the very time God had promised him" (Gen. 21:1–2).

Do you know what I love about those verses? Sarah is the focus. Not Abraham.

All throughout the book of Genesis, God spoke with Abraham about the promises to come. He told Abraham He would make him into a great nation. He told Abraham all the peoples of the earth would be blessed because of that nation—a promise later fulfilled through Jesus Christ. God told Abraham he would have a son. And God told Abraham that son would be born within one year's time.

But look again at Genesis 21:1: "The Lord was gracious to Sarah," and "the Lord did for Sarah what he had promised."

God may have spoken through Abraham, but He knew Sarah. He valued Sarah. He desired greatly to bless Sarah. And He brought His promise to fulfillment by giving Sarah what she desired most.

In the same way, God knows you. God values you. God sees you in the midst of your circumstances, and He wants you to know His promises are true *for you*. The blessings He has promised apply *to you*, and they are coming *for you*.

Don't settle for anything less.

Hope and Joy

It took a little while, but Sarah eventually came to terms with the blessing she received. She understood how God heard her secret whispers and the deepest groanings of her heart. How do I know that? Because of the child's name.

Isaac means "he laughs."

This wasn't the same kind of laughter that had escaped Sarah's lips just a year earlier—the mocking laughter of a bruised and bitter heart. No, this was lighthearted laughter. Slap your knee and smile laughter. The kind of laughter that spreads across a room like a cheerful contagion.

Isn't it wonderful how God can turn our scoffs into hope and our sarcasm into joy?

Holding the child in her arms, Sarah said, "God has brought me laughter, and everyone who hears about this will laugh with me." She added, "Who would have said to Abraham that Sarah would nurse children? Yet I have borne him a son in his old age" (Gen. 21:6–7).

This was a woman whose hope and joy had been restored in a completely unexpected way. What Sarah believed to be dead had been brought back to life—the secret places of her heart were filled again. The smile was back on her face again. The light was back in her eyes again. All because God answered her prayer.

I have felt the joy of unexpected blessings many times in my life. But I especially love it when I see that joy in others. It warms my soul like nothing else.

I have seen women raise their arms in victory and shout for joy when terminal cancer was defeated. I've heard from doctors confused and confounded by scans that showed a metastasizing monster one week and scans that showed nothing but healthy tissue the next.

That's a good feeling. And it happened because of prayer.

I have seen women glow with the joy of relationships restored when everyone they knew told them over and over again that hope was lost. Separation was inevitable. Divorce was a mere formality. I've seen love rekindled and hope restored.

That's a good feeling, too. And it happened because of prayer.

I have seen women find dream jobs when they were convinced they were unqualified. I have seen women receive raises *after* they were told there was no money in the budget and no room for compromise. I have seen women with loans forgiven. I have seen women with foreclosures canceled. I have seen women freed from the fangs of abuse and released from the chains of addiction.

All of it fuels my hope. All of it inspires my joy. And all of it has been made possible because people chose not to settle for what was easy, but to pray for God's promises even when all hope seemed lost.

That is why I will continue to call all women to pray in every circumstance. Because when women pray, they find hope and joy in unexpected places.

CHAPTER 4

The Woman with the Issue of Blood

When women pray, they gain victory over the "issues" of life.

The woman felt the crowd surge around her, and she moved with it. Always sure to keep herself on the outer edge. Always sure to keep her eyes focused on the rabbi coming toward her from the other direction. The teacher. The healer.

This might work, she thought, doing her best to quell the rush of hope in her breast. He was moving closer with each step. *This might work!*

She had been planning this moment for days. Watching from the shadows. Waiting for just the right opportunity. Just the right chance. And now she was closer than she'd ever been.

"Watch it!" She felt the lurch before she heard the words as she bumped into the man in front of her. Not hard. She weighed almost nothing these days. But the man still yelled. He would have yelled much louder if he knew the truth—if he knew her condition.

"Sorry, sir," she muttered, eyes low.

Jehovah, forgive me! she prayed. She knew how the law applied to her condition—none better. She'd been reminded of it constantly for twelve years now. "You must keep the Israelites separate from things that make them unclean, so they will not die in their uncleanness for defiling my dwelling place, which is among them" (Lev. 15:31).

It was a violation for her to touch anyone. She should have kept her distance from the crowd. She should have cried out, "Unclean! Unclean!" whenever she approached another person. She should have told the man about her curse—about the blood. He was legally required to cleanse himself after touching her. But she dare not cause a scene. Not when the teacher was so close.

Forgive me, she prayed again. *I am desperate.*

It was true. Whatever money there had been when the bleeding started, it was gone now. Whatever family she had claimed, they had moved on. Whatever dignity she once carried had long since drained away, buried among the strips of cloth she washed and dried each night to try to hide her shame.

The crowd shifted again, and all of a sudden He was right next to her. He was surrounded by His disciples, but there was a window—small and getting smaller. She could see the swinging tassel on the corner of His robe. *Now or never!*

She felt it as soon as she grasped the tassel—the healing. The gentle fire ran through her belly and both legs, leaving a tingle for a few seconds after. By then she had pulled away from the rabbi and was looking for a gap in the crowd to make her escape.

It worked! It's done! I'm free!

That's when she heard His voice, loud even in the marketplace. Commanding. "Who touched me?" Demanding an answer.

Unable to deny that voice, she turned to face Him. To answer Him.

God help me!

Beyond Issues

The first thing that strikes me about this woman is that we are never told her name.

Luke introduces her this way in his gospel: "And a woman was there who had been subject to bleeding for twelve years, but no one could heal her" (8:43). Mark adds, "She had suffered a great deal under the care of many doctors and had spent all she had, yet instead of getting better she grew worse" (5:26).

This woman was brave. This woman demonstrated a deep and powerful faith in God's power to heal. This is a woman who has been read about, talked about, and preached about literally for centuries—and yet we know almost nothing about her.

Despite her positive qualities, this woman was defined almost entirely by her "issue." By her problem. By her pain.

Did you know the same thing can happen to you? Yes, it can. Because we're all dealing with issues. Every one of us. We're all dealing with pain. We're all dealing with problems that threaten to overwhelm us. We're all dealing with difficult circumstances that will try to define who we are—if we allow them.

Here's a principle: when your "issue" threatens to swallow up even your name, your only hope is prayer.

This woman understood that. And she chose to reach out toward God with all her strength. According to the text, she thought, "If I just touch his clothes, I will be healed" (Mark 5:28). Luke is a little more specific in his reporting: "She came up behind [Jesus] and touched the edge of his cloak, and immediately her bleeding stopped" (8:44).

Why did she touch Jesus' cloak? Specifically, why did she touch "the edge of his cloak"? And why in the world did she believe doing so would bring about her healing?

The answer to each of those questions is that this woman believed the truth of God's Word. In the Old Testament book of Numbers, God commanded the Israelites to wear four-cornered outer garments, and for each of the corners to be decorated with white-threaded tassels. The tassels included a single blue thread, which was a symbol of the wearer's commitment to obey God's laws. Such a garment would have been worn by every Jewish man in the ancient world, and the practice is still observed in many Jewish communities today.

Over the centuries, these tassels came to carry an even greater significance within the Jewish community. People of noble ancestry would add new colors or patterns to their tassels to display their authority. Remember when David cut off a corner of Saul's robe in the Desert of Ein Gedi? He was symbolically cutting off Saul's authority as king. Tassels could also represent a person's role or place within the community—including that of a rabbi. A teacher. A healer.[1]

In short, by grabbing the corner of Jesus' robe, this woman was grabbing for His tassel. She was grabbing hold of Jesus' authority and the symbol of His commitment to God's Word—including the promises of His Word.

What a wonderful picture of prayer! When you are in danger of being swallowed up or defined by your issues, don't complain about it. Don't let yourself get down in the dumps.

Grab hold of God! Grab Him and don't let go.

Know Your Value

There's another lesson we can learn from this woman with the issue of blood: she knew her value in God's eyes. She understood that she was valuable to God and worth His time, and she refused to allow anyone to stand between herself and the healing she was desperate to receive.

You'll notice in both the gospel accounts of her story that this woman was not Jesus' main objective on the day in question. Instead, the text says, "a man named Jairus, a synagogue leader, came and fell at Jesus' feet, pleading with him to come to his house because his only daughter, a girl of about twelve, was dying" (Luke 8:41–42).

First of all, do you think it's a coincidence that the dying girl was twelve years old and the woman had been dealing with her affliction for twelve years? I don't. There are no coincidences when God is in the picture. Indeed, there is a certain poignancy in the juxtaposition of these two people—a young girl in danger of losing her life on the cusp of womanhood, and a woman seeking salvation after her flowering years had been stolen away.

Both of them needed Jesus—and Jesus knew it.

Notice that Jairus, the little girl's father, was "a synagogue leader." That means he was a leader in the local temple. He was a man of importance. He was most certainly a wealthy man. A respected man. A pillar in the community.

Notice also that Jairus had come to Jesus with a legitimate need: his daughter was dying. Like the woman with the issue of blood, doctors had been unable to help. Jairus and his wife had done everything they could think of to save their little girl, but she was slipping away. I can imagine Jairus sprinting through the streets in search of a last hope—this miracle worker named Jesus who made the lame to walk and the blind to see.

Not only was Jairus there, likely surrounded by

some of his servants, but Jesus' disciples were packed close to Him as He walked along the streets. These were a rough group of characters—fisherman and zealots and a tax collector and more. We know on several occasions the disciples tried to prevent people from gaining access to Jesus; they viewed themselves as bouncers tasked with keeping out the riffraff.

Do you know how the society of Jesus' day viewed a woman who had been unclean for twelve years? Riffraff. If the disciples had seen her coming, they likely would have blocked her way. "The teacher is busy with an important man right now. Move along."

None of these factors deterred this courageous woman from enacting her plan to grab hold of God's healing power. I love that. I love her tenacity. Her drive. Her knowledge that this was her only remaining hope and *she was going to take it no matter what.*

Make no mistake: this world will always try to convince you that you're not enough. Not valuable enough. Not respected enough. Not good enough. Not clean enough. Not holy enough. Not financially secure enough. Not socially accepted enough. Not feminine enough. Not smart enough.

You've felt that pull, haven't you? You've had other people try to drag you down and belittle you. Maybe your parents were quick to point out your failures and slow to build up your confidence. Maybe your siblings constantly tried to cut your legs out from under you while you were growing up—maybe they still do. Maybe you have coworkers who seek to increase their job security by boosting your insecurity. Maybe your spouse has a regular way of letting you know when they feel disappointed with you.

Not only that, but our culture has a way of making us feel small. Whenever we turn around, it seems we can't help seeing someone more attractive than we are. We can't help seeing someone with a better house than we have. We can't help seeing someone with a better degree than we earned. We can't help seeing someone with a better vacation than we had. We can't help seeing the very best of every other person on social media, and we can't help comparing those bests with what we know about our own worsts.

It's a recipe for feeling small. For feeling not enough.

Not only that, but we have a spiritual enemy in this world, and he will work overtime to make you believe you're not enough. He wants you to think you're not righteous enough to bring your requests before a holy God. He wants you to believe you're not humble enough if you pray for something you need. He wants you to believe you're not meek enough if you ask God to stand next to you in battle. He wants you to believe you're not joyful enough if you approach God's throne to pour out your despair.

Don't let any of it work. Don't believe a word of it. Because the overwhelming message of God's revelation through Scripture is that you are more than enough.

Paul declared we are "God's chosen people, holy and dearly loved" (Col. 3:12). That's you.

John said we are "children of God" (1 John 3:1). That's you.

Peter said we are "God's elect...chosen according to the foreknowledge of God the Father" (1 Pet. 1:1–2). That's you as well.

The Bible says you are the apple of God's eye. You are His treasured possession. You are cherished. Loved. Sought out. Chosen. You are worth searching for and fighting for. You are worth dying for!

In short, you are valuable to God. Therefore, never allow anything to prevent you from coming to Him in prayer.

Don't Stop

There's one more characteristic I want to highlight about this woman with the issue of blood: she never gave up. She kept working and kept reaching until she had grabbed hold of what she needed. Obviously, this characteristic is critically important when it comes to our prayer lives.

Let's make sure we understand the context for this woman's particular "issue." The Old Testament law included a number of provisions designed to highlight purity and cleanliness in the Israelite community—not "cleanliness" in terms of keeping the floor mopped (although that's important) but moral cleanness. Righteousness.

According to those provisions, people or homes or clothing that were corrupted in any way—that were made unclean—needed to be purified before they could be returned to their normal routines. When something became unclean, there was typically a process for making it clean again, but it took effort. Sometimes a lot of effort. Still, those rules and regulations needed to be followed in order for the community to remain a viable location for God's name to dwell.

One of those provisions specifically mentioned women who experienced bleeding outside of their normal period: "When a woman has a discharge of blood for many days at a time other than her monthly period or has a discharge that continues beyond her period, she will be unclean as long as she has the discharge, just as in the days of her period" (Lev. 15:25). According to this law, when a woman suffered from bleeding of this kind, anything she touched was also considered unclean. That included any chair she sat on, any bed she slept on—and any person she came in contact with.

There were additional consequences for being "unclean" in the culture of Jesus' day. For one thing, such a person was required to announce their condition when they came in proximity to others. They had to walk the streets shouting, "Unclean! Unclean!"

More important, people who were ritually unclean were unable to access the temple. They were unable to worship. They were unable to make sacrifices and receive atonement from sins. Meaning, they were cut off from people and closed off from meaningful access to God.

Here's something I have learned from experience: There is no pain quite like the pain of isolation. There is no sorrow quite like the sorrow of being separated from those you care about and wondering if anybody cares about you in return. There is no despair quite like the despair of feeling unworthy and unappealing and unloved because every time you reach out to connect with someone or draw close to someone, they pull away.

The Woman with the Issue of Blood

The woman with the issue of blood endured social and spiritual isolation for twelve years. I'm sure it felt like a lifetime.

Yet she never gave up.

I'm sure this woman did what so many of us do when we struggle with a debilitating illness. First, she sought out the care and counsel of doctors. She started in her own neighborhood, hopeful that a cure would come quickly. As the months dragged on, she branched out to specialists farther away. She may have walked all the way to Jerusalem, the big city, so she could find the best physicians. That's probably when she lost her money. Drained dry.

When she lost all confidence in the medical personnel of her day, I imagine she tried alternative treatments. She talked with her neighbors and her aunties to see what they recommended. She may have experimented with the ancient equivalent of yoga and homeopathy. Maybe someone convinced her she had been cursed in some way, and she sought in vain for a way to remove what had been pressed upon her.

Later, when all other hopes had faltered and all other avenues ran dry, I imagine she turned to prayer. Perhaps she found a way to offer sacrifices. Perhaps she called out to the priests from a distance— "Intercede for me!" When she removed her unclean clothes at night and lay on her unclean bed, I imagine she pounded her fists against her unclean chest and begged God to remove this burden. To remove this curse. To remove this stain of corruption.

Still, she did not give up.

And when the moment of her deliverance came near, she recognized it. She recognized Him. She had heard the stories for months—a rabbi who restored sight. A teacher who transformed the leper's skin. A healer who held authority even over the demons of Hades.

This woman knew Jesus was her only remaining hope, and she reached for Him with tenacity and aggression. She held nothing back and would not allow herself to be held back.

As a result, she found healing. And not just physical healing.

Look at what the text says about Jesus' reaction to this woman's action: "Then the woman, knowing what had happened to her, came and fell at his feet and, trembling with fear, told him the whole truth. He said to her, 'Daughter, your faith has healed you. Go in peace and be freed from your suffering'" (Mark 5:33–34).

"Daughter."

In a single word, Jesus transformed this woman's identity. No longer was she unclean. No longer was she "not enough." No longer was she cut off and excluded from society. No longer was she identified solely be her "issue."

Now she was a daughter of the King!

The same is true of you, though I understand you may sometimes find that difficult to believe. You are a child of the King, adopted into His family not because you were special or because He needed you, but simply because He wanted you—issues and all.

My sister, you and I both know there is an "issue" dragging you down. It's been there a long time. It's been pulling on you a long time. I don't know what it is, but you do. I don't know what caused it, but you do. I don't know everything you've done to try to remove it or get yourself out from under it in some way, but you know.

Nothing has worked. When you've worked up the courage to talk about your issue with those you trust, they've offered suggestions but no solutions. When you've tried to bring your issue before professionals, they've taken your resources but given no relief. You've read books to try to solve things. You've watched Oprah and Dr. Phil, and maybe Dr. Oz as well. You've listened to your pastor's preaching and your spouse's suggestions. But you're still stuck. You're still burdened.

You're desperate for answers.

I want you to know I've been where you are. I've suffered in a way very similar to what you're experiencing, and I've walked alongside the women I love as they have suffered as well. May I tell you what I've learned through my journey and theirs? Don't stop. Don't give up.

Keep going forward. Keep praying.

No matter how desperate your circumstances may seem right now, there is relief in your future. There is hope in your future. There is healing. So don't stop. Keep praying.

Just like this woman with the issue of blood, do not stop reaching until you've grabbed hold of God. Don't stop stretching until you touch your Savior— He's waiting for you. He's hesitating in that crowd, slowing down right in front of you. Don't stop praying until you hear His voice, because you know what He will say when He looks down and sees the tears streaking down your face? "Daughter, your faith has healed you."

That's what happens when women pray: they find victory over the issues of life.

CHAPTER 5

Naomi

When women pray, curses are turned into blessings.

Naomi recognized the bend in the road ahead. It had been many long years since she'd seen it, but she knew it still. If her eyes had been closed, she probably could have identified this specific turn by the way her footsteps echoed off the rocks and ridges.

Just like when I was a girl, she thought. *I still remember it.*

She was almost home.

"It is good to see you smile, Mother. Are we close?"

The young woman's voice startled Naomi out of her thoughts. "Yes, child," she said. Then she corrected herself. "Yes, Ruth. Once we make the turn ahead, you will see Bethlehem."

Naomi noticed with approval that Ruth's voice was still strong in spite of the day's journey up the rugged slopes through the mountains. She was breathing easily, her steps light and confident. *She is still young*, Naomi thought, *but perhaps I was wrong about her. Perhaps she will find a life here after all.*

The two women drifted back into silence as they approached the curve. *Ruth may yet find life*, Naomi mused, *but that's what I was seeking when I left this place, and look what has happened to me. I found nothing in Moab but death.*

With a start, Naomi realized she had been not much older than Ruth when her young family left Bethlehem. There had been a famine in Israel, and food was beginning to run short. It had been Elimelek's idea to live in Moab for a time. "The children must eat," he had told her. "We will plunder the pagans for a few years and return home with sheep and goats at our sides and rings on our fingers. It will be just like our people plundered the Egyptians in the time of Moses."

Naomi shook her head. *He never ran out of promises.* No matter how difficult the journey, no matter how hard the work, Elimelek always had a plan. He was always quick with promises.

His promises had died with him in Moab. Then all the planning had fallen to her.

"There are no goats by my side, Elimelek," she whispered as they turned the corner. "There are no rings on my fingers, my husband. Even you and our sons are gone."

Ruth looked over for a moment but did not speak. She had become used to her mother-in-law's brooding.

There were no more smiles for Naomi as the road straightened and Bethlehem appeared in front of them. She could see smoke rising from cookfires as women prepared the evening meal. There were twinkles here and there from lamps already ignited against the coming darkness of night.

She was home.

What will they say? she thought. *What will they say when they see what has become of me?*

Under a Curse

We all understand that difficult circumstances are part of life. We all know that trials and tragedies will touch us at some point, and we expect them. We anticipate them. We do our best to be prepared for those moments when they come.

But sometimes the depth and the breadth of those circumstances go way beyond our expectations. Sometimes what we view as a difficult moment can stretch into a season. Not just a struggle, but a season of struggle. Not just a single trial or tragedy, but a season of trials and tragedies.

These seasons come about when suffering and pain seem to stack on top of one another. They multiply. They compound one another. First your husband gets injured in an accident. That's bad. He can't work because of his injury, which means money gets tight—or maybe it runs out and you start that terrifying drift into debt. That's worse. Then your children begin to turn restless and sullen; they stop coming home after school because they don't like seeing Dad sitting useless on the sofa and they're tired of the constant tension. Maybe your son starts hanging out with the wrong crowd. That's worse still. Finally, you get a knock on your front door after midnight. The police have come to tell you there was a fight. There was a gun. And your son won't be coming home.

That's worst of all.

In those seasons when it seems like everything that *can* go wrong *does* go wrong, it's easy to believe life will never be the same. It's easy to believe God has forgotten about you. It's easy to believe you've come under a curse and will never recover.

That's what Naomi believed. That's what she experienced.

Like many women around the world today, Naomi was a refugee. She and her family fled their home to escape a period of famine, settling in a foreign land called Moab. They were searching for a better life. Sadly, they never found it.

First Naomi's husband died. Then, in what was surely a blow to Naomi as a Jewish mother, her sons both married Moabite women in direct disobedience to the Mosaic law. Finally came the cruelest stroke of all when both of Naomi's sons passed away. She was left in a place she did not belong with daughters-in-law she did not desire.

All of this took place over a period of ten years. A season of suffering.

When we look at Naomi's story as a whole, there's an interesting parallel with another character from the Old Testament named Job. In case you don't remember that story, Job was a righteous man who also happened to be the wealthiest and most prosperous person in his region. He had lots of money. He had to hire shepherds and servants to take care of his vast flocks and herds. He even had several sons and daughters with whom he could share his blessings.

Then, one day, Job's world came crashing down. His animals were stolen. His servants and workers were murdered by raiders. His sons and daughters were killed in a natural disaster. Later, Job himself was afflicted with painful sores all over his body.

Job went from the penthouse to the outhouse in less than twenty-four hours, and the experience broke his spirit. He, too, felt like he was under a curse. He said, "May the day of my birth perish, and the night that said, 'A boy is conceived!' That day—may it turn to darkness" (Job 3:3–4). Later he added, "What I feared has come upon me; what I dreaded has happened to me. I have no peace, no quietness; I have no rest, but only turmoil" (vv. 25–26).

Maybe you know from experience how Job felt in that moment. "What I feared has come upon me." You've been there, haven't you? Maybe you're there now. The trap you have dreaded for so long has finally sprung, and like Naomi you feel left with nothing.

Winston Churchill said, "If you're going through hell—keep going." That's good advice, but I would change it a little bit to this: "If you're going through hell, keep praying." Because prayer is what will get you through.

If you've got suffering in your current season of life, I also suggest you keep reading. Because it's critical for you to understand *why* you are experiencing what you are experiencing right now. And it's critical for you to learn how prayer can help you survive until this season is over.

The Enemy's Attack

The reason I'm including Job's story in connection with Naomi is because of how the book of Job pulls back the divine curtain to reveal the source of our seasons of suffering.

Yes, there is a source of our suffering. Did you believe your pain was random? Have you bought into the message of this world that sometimes "stuff happens" for no reason at all? Have you given credence to the claim that all the calamity and all the crises and all the critical situations in this world can be boiled down to nothing more than random chance?

No. There is a source behind our seasons of suffering, and his name is Satan. The devil. Our enemy.

As a leader in the church, I always anticipate the attacks of our enemy. I don't want to say I'm used to it, because each attack is new and each carries a unique element of pain. But I expect such attacks against me. What I hate most, however, is when Satan launches his attacks not directly at me, but against those I love.

I remember when I first moved our family to Dallas. My wife and I were thirty-eight or thirty-nine years old, and this was our first time moving to the big city. Just in terms of driving directions, it was daunting trying to move from place to place in this new city jammed with highways and concrete overpasses and toll roads and everything else.

More than that, Serita and I were doing our best to learn the best ways to manage a new church. Our congregation was active and growing, which was a wonderful blessing. But it was also a major responsibility. We had to hire several new staff members, which meant trying to fulfill complex relational tasks with team members who were strangers. We had to ordain people as deacons who in hindsight were nowhere near ready to be deacons.

I can say with confidence the only way we made it through that season was with the help of my mother-in-law. I thought I was busy at the time, but looking back I can see how Serita was pulled in about a hundred different directions. She had growing kids, a growing church, a new home, an amorous husband, a demanding travel schedule, and a new spotlight that was bigger than anything she'd dealt with before. The only way she was able to handle all that and more was because of her mom, who lived with us during that time.

Serita's mom was a lifeline in many ways. She helped with the kids. She was a confidant to both of us. She was a friend during good times and bad times. She made it possible for Serita and me to do the impossible.

Unfortunately, she was also sick. And we had no idea what was coming.

My wife and I were in Philadelphia when we got the phone call. All these years later, I have no idea what we were doing there—probably a conference of some kind. But I remember clearly the terror in Serita's eyes as she listened to that phone call. Her mother had been rushed to the hospital. She was on life support, and doctors were saying there was little chance she would recover.

We flew home right away, of course. We camped out at the hospital to see her and be with her in those final moments. But I know without a doubt that when they turned off the respirator that was breathing for her mother, something in Serita turned off as well. A part of the life and vibrancy I had always seen and loved in my wife went limp, and I'm not sure it was ever resuscitated.

That was a terrible season in so many ways, and I knew clearly we were under attack. My entire family was under attack. And our only recourse was to pray.

When we read Job's story, we see God pointing out Job as an example of righteousness—a man who was wealthy and blessed, yet remained humble and hard-working and kind. Satan responded to God by asking, "Have you not put a hedge around him and his household and everything he has? You have blessed the work of his hands, so that his flocks and herds are spread throughout the land. But now stretch out your hand and strike everything he has, and he will surely curse you to your face" (1:10–11).

The result was devastating for Job, as we've seen. Yet despite all his losses, Job refused to speaking even a word against God.

Satan doubled down by saying, "Skin for skin!... A man will give all he has for his own life. But now stretch out your hand and strike his flesh and bones, and he will surely curse you to your face" (2:4–5).

The book of Ruth doesn't pull back the curtain in the same way as the book of Job. We can't read about Satan's maneuverings in the background of Naomi's suffering. But make no mistake: he was there. He was dancing at the death of Naomi's husband. He was present when her sons passed away, and he smiled at her pain. He looked with approval as she started her long journey back to Israel, bent and broken on the dusty road.

Satan and his forces are present in your life as well. If you have any connection with God whatsoever, then the devil is your enemy. And he is relentless in his desire for your destruction. I use that word intentionally. He's not out to mess with you. He doesn't want to disturb you. He doesn't care about disrupting you.

He wants to destroy you.

There's bad news and good news when it comes to Satan's influence in our lives. The bad news is that he is stronger than you. Stronger than me. Stronger than any of us.

The Bible says this of Satan: "Your enemy the devil prowls around like a roaring lion looking for someone to devour" (1 Pet. 5:8). The implication is that Satan is capable of devouring us. He was originally created as a mighty angel—the first and best of his kind. He's been around for years upon years, millennia upon millennia, which means he's smarter than us as well. He is deadly dangerous in every way.

Here's an important principle: when you face an enemy stronger than you and smarter than you, your only hope is to pray.

Why pray? Because Satan is not stronger than God. In

fact, Satan remains directly under the authority of God. When Satan wanted to get at Job, he had to come to God for permission and he was required to stay within the limits God set. The same was true when Satan launched his attacks against Naomi, and the same is true when he launched his attacks against you and me.

That's the good news. You and I have the opportunity to be in direct communication with the One who has already conquered our enemy.

There is power in prayer.

Unfortunately, it seems from Scripture that Naomi endured long years in her season of suffering without accessing that power.

A Root of Bitterness

Do you remember the last time you tasted something bitter? I don't like the experience personally, but I'll often get a bitter taste from kale or Brussels sprouts or one of those other green vegetables. I can be munching away on a salad or something, and all of a sudden I'll hit one leaf that just sets my teeth on edge.

In my experience, bitterness is a flavor we rarely enjoy with our meals—and one we never enjoy in our lives.

As we look more closely at Naomi's story, however, we see she was intimately familiar with feelings of bitterness. When her daughters-in-law expressed a desire to accompany her back to Israel, she went into great detail explaining all the reasons they were better off remaining in Moab. "Why would you come with me?" she asked (Ruth 1:11). She described herself as a woman who would never again know the joy of a husband and never again watch her children grow older.

"It is more bitter for me than for you," she told them, "because the Lord's hand has turned against me!" (v. 13).

Isn't it tempting to compare ourselves to others when times are tough? Instead of falling on our faces in prayer, we stand up on a high horse and look out at everyone around us. We tell ourselves, *Nobody has it as bad as I do. All of my friends are on Easy Street compared with what I'm going through.*

There's a perverse pleasure to be found in setting ourselves overtop of everyone else, even when the criteria for our comparison is suffering. But such comparisons are counterproductive. They only suck you further down into your pit.

Later, when Naomi and Ruth reached Bethlehem, those who had known Naomi in the past were shocked to see what had become of her in the present. The women of the town exclaimed, "Can this be Naomi" (v. 19).

First, that's a brutal question to be confronted with in your childhood home. When life hasn't gone the way you planned, it's easy for shame to take root in our hearts. We don't want people to know about our false steps and failures—especially those who remember us during the flower of our youth.

That's why we so often avoid reunions and gatherings of those people from our past. *I can't let them see me now when I used to have such promise and potential.* That's also why we try to put our best foot forward on social media. We only post the pictures that catch us at just the right angle. We only make public those moments that allow us to brag a little. Everything else stays hidden. Locked away.

Second, Naomi's answer to the women of her hometown is heartbreaking:

> "Don't call me Naomi," she told them. "Call me Mara, because the Almighty has made my life very bitter. I went away full, but the Lord has brought me back empty. Why call me Naomi? The Lord has afflicted me; the Almighty has brought misfortune upon me."
> (vv. 20–21)

That name *Mara* means "bitter." These are the words of a woman who has allowed bitterness to consume her identity. These are the words of a woman who has allowed bitterness to consume her heart. And these are the words of a woman who has lost all sense of her own value as a child of God.

The author of Hebrews warned against the destructive power of bitterness, writing, "See to it that no one falls short of the grace of God and that no bitter root grows up to cause trouble and defile many" (Heb. 12:15).

Bitterness is like a root in that it grows deep, down in the places we can't easily see or access. Bitterness has a way of sucking up our hurt and our regret and our sorrow—all the destructive feelings we swim in during seasons of suffering—and then pumping them directly into our hearts. It changes us, withering our hearts and minds from the inside out.

It's bitterness that drives you to feel irritated or even angry at the good fortunes of those around you. When you're down, sometimes it's easier to wish that everyone else were down in the dirt with you rather than making the effort to pray to God and ask Him to lift you up. Make you clean again. Bring you healing.

It's bitterness that drives you to alcohol or drugs or food or pornography or anything else as a method of coping with your season of suffering. When you've been consumed by bitterness, you develop a desire to consume anything that will get the taste out of your mouth—anything that will rinse the sourness from your heart.

It's bitterness that drives you to blame others for the pain you've experienced—and especially to blame God. Naomi said, "The Lord has afflicted me; the Almighty has brought misfortune upon me." It's easy to use God as a punching bag when life is hard, but that is also counterproductive. It solves nothing.

Instead, when we find ourselves in the midst of suffering, we need to fall down on our knees before God's throne and cry out, "Lord Jesus, have mercy on me, a sinner."

Naomi allowed bitterness to take root inside her, and it almost brought her down.

Almost.

Curses to Blessings

If you only read the first chapter of Ruth, it seems like a depressing story. A disheartening story of an old woman so beaten down by life that she literally gets to the end of her road and gives up.

Thankfully, there are three more chapters to Naomi's story—and to Ruth's.

If you're in a season of suffering right now, you need to remember there are more chapters in your life as well. You've still got more story in your story! You've still got more life in your life! So don't give up. Don't allow yourself to be consumed by bitterness or filled with regret. There's more to come for you.

I mentioned earlier that Naomi likely was not pleased when her son chose Ruth as a wife. That didn't have much to do with Ruth as a person; rather, it was based on Ruth's identity as a Moabite. Jewish men were supposed to marry Jewish women—that was what God Himself had commanded when He gave the law to Moses. Therefore, Ruth's presence was likely a bone of contention in Naomi's household.

It's ironic, then, that Ruth is the only one who stood by Naomi's side through that season of suffering. No matter how low Naomi went, Ruth was there. No matter how much Naomi complained, Ruth was there. And no matter how much Naomi lashed out or wished for better, Ruth was there to see her through.

More than that, there's a double irony at play in this story because Ruth was ultimately the spark for Naomi's salvation.

In the Israelite community, bloodlines were

everything. They were critical not only for building a family name, but also for the inheritance of property through generations. Therefore, the fact that Naomi's sons were dead meant her husband's name and property rights would be passed on to another. She was the end of the line for her family.

The only hope was in an obscure regulation in Jewish law that allowed for a "kinsman redeemer." This was a man within an extended family who could be given the option of helping his family members who were in great need—including the need to extend that family's lineage by producing a new heir.

Basically, a kinsman redeemer could step in as a replacement husband.

The problem in Naomi's situation was Naomi herself. She was an older woman, which meant she was probably past the point of no return when it came to conceiving a child. Also, her age made it more difficult when it came to convincing the kinsman redeemer in her family to enjoy the privileges of his position—if you know what I mean.

Ruth, though, was a different matter.

Sure enough, with Naomi's guidance, Ruth attracted the attention of the kinsman redeemer in Naomi's family—a man named Boaz. The two were joined as husband and wife, and they later produced a son. That meant Naomi's family line would continue. She would not be destitute. She would not be abandoned. She would not be forgotten (or worse, disparaged) by those who came after her in the community.

Instead, she was blessed.

In fact, listen to what Naomi's neighbors said about her once the child was born:

> The women said to Naomi: "Praise be to the Lord, who this day has not left you without a guardian-redeemer. May he become famous throughout Israel! He will renew your life and sustain you in your old age. For your daughter-in-law, who loves you and who is better to you than seven sons, has given him birth." (Ruth 4:14–15)

The people of Bethlehem praised the Lord because of the birth of a child. Sound familiar?

As with Sarah, none of Naomi's prayers are recorded in Scripture. But God understood the secret whispers of her heart. Just like you, Naomi yearned to be through her season of suffering. She longed to let go of the shame and the bitterness that had coagulated in her heart. She desired a life of significance and purpose.

Do you know the best part of Naomi's story? Here it is: "The women living there said, 'Naomi has a son!' And they named him Obed. He was the father of Jesse, the father of David" (v. 17).

Ruth was the grandmother of King David. Which means Naomi was his great-grandmother. It's even possible she held him in her arms—pressed his cheek against her own. That also means Naomi was legally part of the lineage of Christ. Not only was she blessed when her family line was restored, but all the peoples of the earth have been blessed through her as well.

That's why you must not let bitterness and grief overwhelm you during seasons of sorrow—because you never know what God has planned for your future. You may have kings living in you! You may be the instrument God is honing and shaping to be used in just the right way to produce a blessing unlike your city or your community has ever seen.

I'll say it again: If you're going through hell, keep going. And keep praying. Because when women pray, curses are turned into blessings.

CHAPTER 6

The Samaritan Woman

*When women pray, they are quenched
of their thirst.*

It was the heat she hated most.

Yes, the jar was heavy, especially once it was filled with water. But she was getting stronger. She was beginning to feel the weight less. A little, anyway. And yes, the journey was long. After three or four trips she walked with a limp the rest of the day because of the pain in her feet, but that was manageable. A small price.

But the heat was different. The full weight of the sun pressing down on her—baking down on her—was a heavy burden. Heavier than the water. The intensity of the light stung her eyes going one direction and seared her neck and shoulders going back. Taken together, the whole experience was beginning to feel unbearable.

No, she thought. *It is not unbearable, because I know I will continue to bear it.*

The other women drew their water together in the cool of the morning. They chatted as they walked, exchanging pleasantries and the latest gossip while the sun was just beginning to peek out over the mountains. They worked together to pull the heavy jars up from the bottom of the well, dripping and sloshing as they pulled the rope, so that no one was overwhelmed by the load.

She used to join them, but no longer. She grew tired of the knowing looks they passed back and forth whenever they mentioned their husbands. With every cutting comment—such sweetness and sharpness from so many tongues—her fury had grown, threatening to overflow like one of their jars. "I saw your second husband at the market yesterday—or was it your third?" "I know Rachel wanted to invite you to her wedding, dear, but she thought you might be uncomfortable."

That had become unbearable. Truly unbearable.

She relished the quiet in the middle of the day. No other women. No one to help her, that was true, but no one to confront her, either. No one to offer rebuke and rejection under the pretense of kindness.

Still, she cursed the heat.

Several hundred yards from the well, she stopped. Someone was sitting on it. Resting. Waiting? *Will they give me no peace?* she thought. *Have they left someone to stab at me even now in the heat of the day?*

But no. As she drew closer, she realized the person sitting was too large to be a woman. Too thick. Too strong. It was a man.

But why would a man be here? she thought. *And why now?*

What could he possibly want?

Hiding Away

In the fourth chapter of John's gospel, we find another Bible character who is both nameless and famous. You may have heard this particular woman described as "the Samaritan woman" or "the woman at the well."

Unlike the woman with the issue of blood, this woman did not seek out Jesus. She wasn't looking for Jesus. In fact, she wasn't looking for anyone—quite the opposite. She was trying to hide. She was laying low.

Hunkering down. Doing her best to remain anonymous and unseen.

Fortunately for her, Jesus wasn't having any part of it. He had come specifically to find her and to provide for her in ways she could not yet understand.

Just as He does for you and me.

We know this woman was hiding because the text says that when Jesus sat down at Jacob's well to rest, "it was about noon." Just in case you haven't been to a desert anytime recently, I can tell you it gets hot in the desert. Especially "about noon." And especially in the Middle East. The sun is relentless. You can't escape it, nor can you evade its heat.

Yet that was the time when this woman visited this well to draw water. And just to make sure we are on the same page, this woman carried her heavy jar from her home all the way along a dusty, foot-worn track to the well—to the place where water was available. Then she attached her jar to the rope and lowered it down the shaft until it submerged into the aquifer. When the jar was full, she began the difficult task of heaving that rope and pulling the now heavier jar back up the surface. Struggling to spill as little water as possible, she wrestled the jar up onto her shoulder, or maybe directly on top of her head, and then began the journey back toward town.

If that sounds like a difficult way to get water, remember this: the woman needed water not only for herself, and not only for the man she lived with and any children in the household, but also for any animals they owned. Whatever flocks and herds they managed needed to be fed and watered as well. Daily.

Here's the point: one jar didn't cover all those needs. This woman made several journeys back and forth, back and forth, back and forth. All the time lugging that heavy jar. All the time sweating in her robes and her head covering under the intensity of Israel's sun. She did this day after day, week after week, month after month.

What I am saying is that this woman intentionally endured great hardship and great frustration for a specific purpose: she was hiding from her community. She did not want to join the other women who gathered water in the cool of the morning. She wanted isolation. She wanted solitude. She willingly chose a more difficult path in the present so that she could hide from her past.

We do the same today. We make the same effort to hide away the parts of ourselves or the moments from our past we deem to be inappropriate for public view.

We hide in our cars on isolated commutes. We hide behind office doors or under our headphones. We hide behind the banality of fruitless, friendly conversation. "How are you?" "I'm fine—just enjoying this lovely weather." We hide behind the aura of accomplishment and competence we continually thrust in front of our faces like a shield. We hide behind makeup and hair dye. We hide behind garage doors and social calendars.

Many of us are experts at hiding in plain sight. People see us. They talk with us. They know our favorite sports teams and our hobbies. But they have no idea who we are under the surface. They have no idea what makes us tick or how our past experiences have formed us and shaped us.

In other words, they don't know the real *us* down inside—and we do everything possible to keep it that way.

Hiding from God

Notice that the Samaritan woman attempted to hide from Jesus as well. First, she tried to hide behind a veneer of hostility. When Jesus asked for a drink from the well, she snapped back, "You are a Jew and I am a Samaritan woman. How can you ask me for a drink?" (John 4:9).

Sometimes people who have been hurt are the hardest people in the world to help. Have you noticed that? When you reach out to lend a hand, they smack it away with an attitude. They puff up like a cat, snarling and ready to scratch.

I can tell you from experience that nobody fights harder than someone who is drowning—so you better be prepared if you plan to attempt a rescue. Even when your intentions are good, their desperation can be so bad that they just lash out without thought. You can get killed trying to help somebody who's hurting, and that's the dynamic Jesus encountered at Jacob's well.

As modern readers, we have the benefit of the entire story. We know Jesus intentionally sought out this specific interaction with this specific woman. The text says Jesus "had to go through Samaria" (v. 4). That's a potentially confusing translation, because there was no physical or geographical reason for Jesus to travel through Samaria. In fact, the Jews and the Samaritans were cultural enemies. They did not like one another, and they preferred to avoid one another. For that reason, Jews rarely traveled through Samaria.

Jesus, however, *chose* this particular route. He chose to penetrate enemy territory specifically because He was on a mission to converse and connect with this woman. He was on a mission to save her from drowning.

Not only that, but Jesus sent the disciples away to prepare the ground for that conversation. The text says Jesus was alone because "His disciples had gone into the town to buy food" (v. 8). Remember, there were twelve disciples at this time, and I can tell you from experience it doesn't take twelve men to go get lunch. All it takes is one. Two at the most. "Peter, do me a favor and grab some takeout so we can have a nice meal at this well. Take John with you if you need an extra set of hands."

Why did Jesus send all the disciples away? Because He didn't want them in the way. These were the same fools who had already shouted down blind Bartimaeus when he tried to approach Jesus. They were the same men who shooed children away from the Lord. The same men who would later try to send fire and brimstone down on a group of Samaritans when they rejected Jesus' teachings.

What I'm saying is Jesus went to a great deal of effort to prepare the ground for a significant conversation between Himself and this woman. And instead of recognizing that effort—instead of recognizing her opportunity—the woman at the well tried to push Jesus away because He was different.

How often do we hide behind our differences as a way of ignoring one another? As a way of refusing to get to know one another? *There's no way I'm going to reach out to that person; we don't have anything in common. We came from different backgrounds. We live in different communities. We were raised in different cultures by parents of different colors. We don't look the same or talk the same or think the same or vote the same, therefore there's no reason to make any effort at connection.*

It's all a veneer. A screen. A way to hide behind our differences so we're not confronted with our own prejudices. With our own immaturity.

Later in their conversation, the Samaritan woman attempted to hide from Jesus by distracting Him with theology. When Jesus pointed out some information from her past He had no business knowing—namely, that she had five husbands in her past and was now living with a man who was not her husband—she suddenly became a Bible scholar.

"Sir," the woman said, "I can see that you are a prophet. Our ancestors worshiped on this mountain, but you Jews claim that the place where we must worship is in Jerusalem" (vv. 19–20).

She was describing an ancient dispute between the Jews and the Samaritans. About nine hundred years before Jesus' day, Solomon built the original temple in Jerusalem, which is also called Mount Zion. Hundreds of years later, the Samaritans—who were transplanted to the nation of Israel and who worshiped foreign gods—built a competing temple to worship God on Mount Gerizim. So, there were two competing systems of worship and two competing temples where that worship was concentrated.

In other words, this woman didn't want to answer Jesus' questions, so she tried to hide behind a doctrinal dispute.

Oh, how silly we seem when we try to hide from God. Adam and Eve tried it after they first sinned in the garden, but God wasn't fooled. David thought he had hidden his rebellion from God when he sinned by forcibly taking Bathsheba to his bed and arranging for the murder of her husband, but God wasn't fooled. He sent the prophet Nathan to expose everything that had been done. Jonah tried to hide from God in the belly of a ship bound for Tarshish, but God saw him and sent him down into the belly of a whale.

This is a lesson we all must learn: There is no hiding from God. There are no secrets between yourself and God. There is no distracting Him from seeing all the things you prefer to keep shrouded about your past. There is no confusing Him about knowing all the thoughts that swim around in your mind and heart—those thoughts you try to keep hidden even from yourself.

God knows. He always knows. He always sees.

Therefore, this is a principle I hope you will take to heart: When you come before God in prayer, come honestly. Come openly. Come prepared to acknowledge all the ways you have rebelled against Him and all the times you have been focused on yourself. Because He already knows.

Not only that, He's already made provision to forgive you. He's already mapped out a special trip just to meet you and talk with you—just to heal you and save you, if you'll open your heart and accept what He offers.

Living Water

The one element we haven't yet discussed regarding this Samaritan woman—this woman at the well—is the element that most defines her story.

I'm talking about her thirst.

After His initial request for a drink and the woman's less than gracious reply, Jesus said something that seems out of the blue: "If you knew the gift of God and who it is that asks you for a drink, you would have asked him and he would have given you living water" (v. 10).

The woman was confused, and rightfully so! "Sir," she said, "you have nothing to draw with and the well is deep. Where can you get this living water? Are you greater than our father Jacob, who gave us the well and drank from it himself, as did also his sons and his livestock?" (vv. 11–12).

The woman had a vague understanding that Jesus was making a bold claim—that He was claiming to be somebody. So, she reached back to the past in order to set up a comparison. They were conversing at Jacob's well, after all, so she used Jacob as a sort of measuring stick. A ruler. *Do you think you're greater than Jacob, whose work and provision has brought water to our community for hundreds of years?*

What the woman did not realize—indeed, what she could not have realized at this point in the conversation—is that Jesus Himself is a wellspring of life. Jesus Himself is a fountain of hope and goodness and provision.

In other words, she did not understand that she was talking to a Well sitting on a well.

Jesus said to her, "Everyone who drinks this water

will be thirsty again, but whoever drinks the water I give them will never thirst. Indeed, the water I give them will become in them a spring of water welling up to eternal life" (vv. 13–14). This was an unmistakable offer of incredible value. This was Jesus Himself offering Himself.

Next came the crux of their conversation. The pivotal moment. The woman answered by saying, "Sir, give me this water so that I won't get thirsty and have to keep coming here to draw water" (v. 15).

My sister, may I submit to you that there is no purer expression of prayer than what that woman asked of Jesus in that moment? "Sir, give me this water."

That is the essence of prayer!

After all, what is prayer but recognizing our own emptiness and asking God to fill us with what we need? "Lord God, I have been searching for acceptance for so long in so many places. Please give me Your acceptance." "Lord God, I have been trying to find love for longer than I can express. Please give me Your love." "Lord God, I am in need of joy and peace and comfort and purpose and blessing. Please give me what I need."

In short, prayer is simply saying, "Lord, I am thirsty. Please fill me with Yourself."

Notice that Jesus exposes the futility of this woman's efforts to quench her own thirst—and he wasn't just talking about physical thirst here. He wasn't just talking about water and wells. This was a woman with five husbands in her rearview mirror. This was a woman living with a man she had not married in a culture where she could legally be stoned to death for such a choice.

This woman had a thirst for companionship. She had a thirst for relationship. She had a thirst to be loved, which is a thirst we all experience. It's a thirst we all share. But she had been trying to quench that thirst in all the wrong places and all the wrong ways.

Make no mistake, the devil always has solutions for your thirst. The devil will always show you different ways to get your needs met. But he's a liar. He wants to devour you. His goal is your destruction.

This world is filled with solutions for your thirst. The economy of our culture is built on inflaming every kind of thirst inside you and then selling you false promises to quench those thirsts. Don't believe those promises. All that glitters is not gold. Just because it winks at you doesn't mean it's a blessing. Just because it feels good doesn't mean it won't harm you in the long run. Just because it makes sense to everyone else doesn't mean it's the right choice for you.

Jesus wanted to show this woman a better way. Himself. The Living Water.

And Jesus wants to show you a better way as well. Because He knows you are thirsty.

God knows you are thirsty for approval. God knows you are thirsty for a career that fulfills you rather than making you feel drained. God knows you are thirsty for someone to love you in a way that makes you feel alive again. God knows you are thirsty for the laughter of children in your house. God knows you are thirsty for the education you had to abandon when you were young. God knows you are thirsty for just one month—or maybe an entire year—where all the bills are paid and there is food on the table and you don't have to feel so squeezed because there is more than enough.

God knows you are thirsty. He is the Well sitting on a well, and He is able to quench your thirst. He wants to quench your thirst! The question is, will you let Him?

Sometimes we get so down on ourselves and beat ourselves up because we've made mistakes in the past. We try to hide because we are ashamed at the choices we made yesterday—maybe some of the choices we made today. Perhaps you even believe you don't deserve what God is offering. You think you don't deserve to have your thirst quenched and be filled with the Living Water of Jesus.

Let me say this in case you need to hear it: desperate people do desperate things. That's a truth I have seen not only as a pastor, not only as a community leader, not only as a husband and a father—that's a truth I have lived myself. You don't have to be evil to make bad choices. You don't have to be wicked to do wicked things. Sometimes you're just desperate.

Thirsty people are desperate people. We need water in our bodies, or else we die. We can only live for so long without it, which makes us desperate. In the same way, we need the Living Water in our souls. We can only live so long without God filling up our spirit before we become desperate. And when we get desperate, we do things we said we would never do. We reach out to places we never expected to go. When we get desperate, we open ourselves up to corruption and rebellion and sin because it feels like the only way to slake the thirst burning inside us.

But there's a better way. Jesus is the Living Water. He is the Bread of Life. And He will provide exactly what you need when you reach out to Him in prayer.

"Lord Jesus, please give me Your water so that I never thirst again."

Many Believe

As we bring this chapter to a close, let me ask you a question: If you were called to bring the good news of salvation to the Samaritan people of Jesus' day, how would you have done it? If you were a Jewish person called to carry the gospel to a people who had been your enemies for generations, what would be your first step?

If it were me, I would have set up an appointment with the magistrates and leaders of the community. The people in authority. At the very least, I would have sought out some of the priests the Samaritan woman mentioned—those who worshiped on Mount Gerizim near Jacob's well. I could open the Scriptures and show them why God directed Solomon to build His temple on Jerusalem. I could help them see the error of their ways.

Or, if it were today, maybe I would launch a website and start a call to action. I could build a platform through social media and recruit others to my cause—#SaveSamaria. I could even try to find some celebrities to weigh in and throw around their influence on my behalf.

But Jesus did none of those things there at Jacob's well in Samaria. He did not meet with the local aristocracy. He did not seek out common ground with the religious leaders.

Instead, Jesus sat on a well and waited for one specific woman to draw near. Because she was thirsty.

I love what the scripture says in John 4: "Then, leaving her water jar, the woman went back to the town and said to the people, 'Come, see a man who told me everything I ever did. Could this be the Messiah?' They came out of the town and made their way toward him" (vv. 28–29).

Why did she leave her water jar? Because she'd found something better.

Look what happened next:

> Many of the Samaritans from that town believed in him because of the woman's testimony, "He told me everything I ever did." So when the Samaritans came to him, they urged him to stay with them, and he stayed two days. And because of his words many more became believers.
>
> They said to the woman, "We no longer believe just because of what you said; now we have heard for ourselves, and we know that

this man really is the Savior of the world."
(vv. 39–42)

We don't know her name, but this woman defined all
her life by her thirst became the instrument through
which God satisfied the thirsts of others. This woman
who came to Jacob's well alone because she had been
shunned by her community became a living well
herself—a tributary of God's grace overflowing with
life-giving water to that same community.

That's why I want to see millions of women praying
in their cities and their towns across the world today.
Because when women pray, they are quenched of their
thirst—and they open up God's springs of blessing so
that entire communities are quenched as well.

CHAPTER 7

Esther

*When women pray, they gain
victory over injustice.*

Esther knew something was wrong as soon as she walked through the door. For one thing, Mordecai was home, though it was not yet time for the evening meal. Typically her cousin and guardian returned late each evening because of his duties at the palace.

More troubling was the presence of the second man. One she had never met. He was a Persian—that was obvious by his dress and the complexion of his skin. He was also a man of authority. One to whom even Mordecai showed deference.

"Hello, Hadassah," Mordecai said, standing to greet her. He always called her by her Hebrew name.

Esther bent at the knees and angled her head toward both men. A show of respect. "I am pleased to see you, my father," she answered, using the honorific title given the present company.

"This is Master Hegai," said Mordecai, gesturing to the stranger. He had not risen, nor had he offered any greeting. "He is—" her cousin hesitated for a moment before finishing. "He is a servant of the king."

Esther bowed her head again in the direction of this newcomer. *Another servant from the palace*, she thought. *Perhaps he works with Mordecai? Perhaps they are here on business?*

"Blessings upon you—" she started the customary greeting, but her words failed at the intensity of Hegai's gaze. He was staring at her openly. Nakedly. First at her face, then down the length of her torso and legs, then back again to linger on her breasts. He said nothing. He did not smile or leer.

He just looked. And kept looking.

Sensing the rising alarm in his young ward, Mordecai reached out to take her hand. "There is news from the palace," he said. "The king has ordered a search be made to find a replacement for Vashti. Hegai is in charge of that search."

Vashti, Esther thought. *The old queen?* She tore her eyes away from the stranger long enough to look at Mordecai, confused. She tried to ask a question with her eyes: *What does this have to do with me?*

"Hadassah." Mordecai's face was kind as always, but there was a gravity to it now. A seriousness she seldom witnessed. "You have been chosen as one of the women to participate."

Esther held his gaze—much better than looking again at this gawking stranger. "Participate?" she asked. "Chosen to help find the new queen?"

"No, my child." Hegai spoke for the first time. His voice was not cold or unfriendly, but there was no warmth to it. It was not the kind of voice Esther was used to hearing from men. He rose from his seat as he spoke again.

"You have been chosen to possibly *be* the next queen."

The Right Stuff

In recent years, I have observed a new class of women taking center stage in many key positions in society. These women seem to rise easily and effortlessly through the ranks. They have an instinctive awareness of what it takes to climb the ladder of success, and they unashamedly aspire to reach the top.

When you encounter these women, you immediately notice their self-confidence and self-assurance. They like the way they look, but they don't feel the need to put other women down. They trust themselves and rely on their own intelligence without belittling those around them. And they are typically so unpretentious and so uninterested in cattiness that even women who are prone to jealousy seek them out as trusted friends.

In another era, we would have said such women have all the right stuff.

Esther was that kind of woman. As a teenager, she was drafted into an *American Idol*-style competition to find the next queen of Persia. Or maybe it was more like *Survivor*. Can you imagine hundreds of young women being thrown together for months under a palace roof, all vying and competing and scratching to become royalty? I shudder at the thought!

Not Esther, though. Seemingly without even trying, Esther rose above the competition. She became queen over the most powerful empire of her day—and she likely did so before she reached her fifteenth birthday.

No wonder Esther's name in the Persian language meant "star."

One of the most surprising elements of Esther's

ascension is that she started from the bottom. She was no pampered princess who had been primped and preened from her youth. Instead, both of Esther's parents passed away when she was still a child. She was an orphan. Not only that, Esther was an immigrant. She was a Jewish girl living in the capital city of the empire that had crushed her ancestors and taken them captive.

In other words, Esther knew what it was like to be different. To be viewed as different. To be scorned as an outsider—someone who wasn't the same color as the majority and didn't hold the same values as the culture around her.

With those disadvantages, how did Esther succeed? Well, she did have three advantages that helped transform her from an orphan into a shooting star. The first was her cousin Mordecai, who adopted her when her parents died. Reading the book of Esther, it's clear that Mordecai was a man of faith. A man of principle. A man who understood right and wrong, and who had the patience and the kindness to teach those same values to his adopted daughter.

The second advantage was Esther's physical attractiveness. Scripture says she "had a lovely figure and was beautiful" (Esther 2:7). I'm sure much of this had to do with Esther's physical features—her hair, her eyes, her curves, and so on. But the idea of attraction is always more complicated than simple body types. Esther was the kind of woman who attracts the attention of others. If she was walking by you on the street, she would catch your eye. There was something "extra" about her that people found attractive.

Perhaps this something extra was connected to Esther's third advantage in life, which was her ability to produce "favor" in others. She was "favor-able." The text says, "Esther won the favor of everyone who saw her" (v. 15). Men and women, young and old, palace guard or street urchin—people simply enjoyed being around Esther. They liked her company. Rather than producing envy or strife in others, she produced favor.

That included the king, whose name was Xerxes: "Now the king was attracted to Esther more than to any of the other women, and she won his favor and approval more than any of the other virgins. So he set a royal crown on her head and made her queen instead of Vashti" (v. 17).

I have met several modern-day Esthers in recent years. These women excel in the classroom and often rise quickly to the boardroom. They are doctors and lawyers. They are the producers of television shows— the people who get things done and keep things interesting day after day, month after month. They are influencers in the very best sense of the word.

Thankfully, we are living in a time when modern-day Esthers are taking their place on the political stage in greater and greater numbers. In the United States, the elections of 2018 resulted in the most diverse Congress in history, with record numbers of women and minorities taking office. That included many younger women, such as Lauren Underwood from Illinois, Haley Stevens from Michigan, and Alexandra Ocasio-Cortez from New York. We are also living in a time when ten of America's one hundred largest cities are run by women, including Keisha Lance Bottoms in Atlanta.

Internationally, many countries have long since surpassed America in terms of government representation by women. I was proud to see Rwanda at the top of that list, where women make up 62 percent of the national legislature.

Certainly there is a long way to go in my own country and many other places around the world, but progress should be celebrated.

Back to modern-day Esthers. There is a particular danger you face when everything goes your way in life. There is a specific trap you can fall into when you have that gift of producing "favor" in those you meet.

Esther was confronted by that trap, and it almost closed around her to produce destruction. Almost! My hope in exploring her story—not to mention the larger message of this book—is that I can help successful young women avoid that same trap today.

The Favor Trap

At Mordecai's request, Esther did not reveal her Jewish heritage when she became queen. She kept her past on the down low and concentrated on the present.

That's not to say Esther wasn't busy. Her time as queen began when the king threw a lavish banquet and invited all his nobles and officials. They called it "Esther's banquet." And don't let that word fool you. A *banquet* today is a temporary event—it's a fancy party that lasts for a few hours, tops. That wasn't the case in the ancient world. This party likely kept going for weeks. And it was all in Esther's honor.

Then there was the matter of Esther's official transition out of the harem and into the palace. She needed a new wardrobe. New shoes. New servants. She began her training in whatever official duties were expected from the queen in those days. She also began deepening her relationship with her new husband.

In short, life was good for this "star" among the women of Persia. Each day was sweeter than the one before, and her future was bright.

What Esther did not realize is that a trap had been laid for her people in the land of their enemies—an evil plot with a sinister foundation and deadly intent.

That plot started with a man named Haman, who was second in command to King Xerxes. Everyone in the capital city had been commanded to bow down to Haman whenever he passed by, but one person refused to do so: Mordecai. As a result, Haman determined to extract revenge:

> When Haman saw that Mordecai would not kneel down or pay him honor, he was enraged. Yet having learned who Mordecai's people were, he scorned the idea of killing only Mordecai. Instead Haman looked for a way to destroy all Mordecai's people, the Jews, throughout the whole kingdom of Xerxes. (Esther 3:5–6)

If you find it a little extreme to commit genocide just because one man doesn't bow to you, I agree. But there was more to the story—a deeper history.

Specifically, the text describes Haman as an "Agagite." That's important. Because when you look way back in the Old Testament, you find an ancient conflict between the Jews and a group of people called

the Amalekites. They were bitter enemies. The Amalekites raided and ransacked the Jews after the exodus
from Egypt. Much later, the Jewish armies under King
Saul sought revenge by routing the Amalekites and
capturing their king.

Can you guess the name of that king? It was Agag—
one of Haman's ancestors. First Samuel 15 tells the
story of Samuel the prophet putting Agag to death in
obedience to God's command.

So, what we see in the interaction between Mordecai and Haman is generational hatred. It's the com-
bination of long-seated prejudice and deeply rooted
antagonism, and it was breaking out all around Esther
without her even realizing it.

Let me pause for a moment and suggest that prayer
is a critical tool for unraveling not only the kind of
generational hatred we see in this story but also the
racial conflict we have experienced across our world
in recent centuries.

No matter where you look on this planet, there are
people who have been defined for generations by their
hatred of other people. Wars have been fought because
of ignorance and prejudice, sometimes stretching
over decades. Nations and economies have been built
through the plunder and exploitation of other nations
and economies. Even in societies such as America

where people of all races are encouraged to live freely and respect one another, the fractures and fault lines of past failures still run deep—and still rumble more often than we like to admit.

None of these problems can be solved overnight. The world requires healing, and it takes generations to heal from generational damage. But if you want to see peace and mutual appreciation among all peoples and nations, as I do, then you ignore the healing power of prayer at your peril.

Esther understood that truth—eventually. But she needed a kick in the pants from Mordecai before she got there.

You see, Haman's plot wasn't the trap I mentioned that had been laid down for Esther. No, what she faced in that moment of her story is what I call the favor trap.

You can catch the subtle edges of that trap when Mordecai asked Esther to intercede with the king on behalf of her people, and she answered with reluctance. With hesitation. "All the king's officials and the people of the royal provinces know that for any man or woman who approaches the king in the inner court without being summoned the king has but one law: that they be put to death unless the king extends the gold scepter to them and spares their lives," she told her adoptive father. "But thirty days have passed since I was called to go to the king" (4:11).

Basically, Esther told Mordecai the king might kill her if she went over to knock on his door. Xerxes hadn't come around to her side of the bed for a month now, and she didn't think it was a good idea to bother him. Maybe she'd try something later when he was in a better mood.

Now, remember who Esther was talking to. She had been living in the palace a few months at this point, but Mordecai had been a faithful servant of the king *for years*. He knew the regulations. He knew the customs. He had already proven his love for Esther, and he knew exactly what she would be risking if she interceded with the king—and he asked her to do it anyway. Because their people were desperate.

The bottom line is that Esther didn't want to get involved. Life was good. She was comfortable. She had reached the top of her world, and whatever she might say about not wanting to lose her life, in reality she was much more worried about losing her position. Her favor. Her blessing.

That is the favor trap, and it can be deadly for any person who has been fortunate enough to achieve success. Why? Because when everything is going well in your life, there will always be a temptation to elevate maintaining your comfort over fulfilling your purpose.

This trap is especially dangerous for women today—the modern-day Esthers. Take it from me: you won't always have the right stuff. Sooner or later you will be tested, just as Esther was tested by Mordecai's request. Sooner or later your attractiveness and your confidence and your favor will not be enough to see you through.

If your career has led you to the pinnacle of your field, there will be a moment of testing when you will be forced to put your corner office and your mahogany desk on the line. You will have to choose between what you've achieved and what you know to be right.

If you are in a season of relational bliss—you've found just the right partner who compliments you and complements you in ways you never thought possible—there will come a moment of testing. You will have to choose whether your relationship with God or your relationship with that partner will occupy top priority in your heart.

If your finances have reached a level of abundance you never dreamed possible, there will be a moment of testing when God stretches out His arm to evaluate your heart. Jesus Himself said we cannot serve two masters—we must choose between God and money.

Rest assured, then, that at some point He will make you choose.

In short, if you have climbed ladders and jumped over fences and lived in the favor of God's blessing, that is a wonderful gift. That is nothing to be ashamed of in any way. But there is a test coming. There is an evaluation on the way.

And if all you can rely on in that moment of testing is your own skill and your own natural charm and attractiveness—you will fail the test. You need something more.

Specifically, you need prayer.

A One-Two Punch

When Mordecai heard the way Esther was waffling about stepping up to help her people, he knew what was going on. He understood the test she was facing, and he understood the danger involved—both for the Jews and for Esther personally.

So, he gave her the kick in the pants she needed:

When Esther's words were reported to Mordecai, he sent back this answer: "Do not think that because you are in the king's house you alone of all the Jews will escape. For if you remain silent at this time, relief and deliverance for the Jews will arise from another place, but you and your father's family will perish. And who knows but that you have come to your royal position for such a time as this?" (4:12–13)

This is a principle we need to understand in today's world: when God opens the windows of heaven and pours out a blessing on you, there's always a reason why. God loves you and genuinely desires your happiness, but there's always more involved with His blessings than simply filling your bank account or blowing up your social media.

What Mordecai wanted Esther to see is that God-given blessings include God-assigned responsibility. He has a purpose in mind. He's given you something so that you can make use of it for His glory, not for your own.

In other words, you have been blessed so you can be a blessing. You have been extended favor so you can reflect that same favor on others.

Fortunately for Esther, Mordecai's wisdom helped her find the right direction:

Then Esther sent this reply to Mordecai: "Go, gather together all the Jews who are in Susa, and fast for me. Do not eat or drink for three days, night or day. I and my attendants will fast as you do. When this is done, I will go to the king, even though it is against the law. And if I perish, I perish." (4:15–16)

I love Esther's plan because it offered a one-two punch against the enemies of her people—and I'm not just talking about Haman and his goons, but also their spiritual enemy, Satan.

The first punch was prayer. That's the left-handed jab in our spiritual warfare. It keeps the enemy off guard. Her second punch was fasting. That's the over-hand right—the knockout swing fueled by the Holy Spirit.

I know a lot of people are uncomfortable at the idea of fasting. Many others are confused about what it is and why they should do it. Entire books have been written on the subject, but let me simply point out that fasting is temporarily abstaining from something physical so you can concentrate on the spiritual. It is removing something of small significance from your life for a time so that you will have extra focus and extra emphasis on that which is eternal.

Historically, fasting has most often been associated with food. The idea is to avoid physical nourishment for a predetermined amount of time—anywhere from a single meal to forty days—so that you can receive a greater portion of spiritual nourishment. Fasting goes hand-in-hand with prayer because of how our bodies work. We are used to eating regularly, of course. So when we voluntarily go without food, our bodies are slow to get with the program. They send out little reminders, both mental and physical. You get that rumble in your belly, and then that mental alarm in the back of your mind that says, *Time to eat!* Instead of eating, however, you simply use those physical and mental sensations as reminders to pray.

Notice also that Esther did not embark on this battle alone. She recruited an entire nation of people to join her in prayer and fasting.

I often wonder why so many Christians in the church today believe prayer to be a solo sport. Why do so many of us believe we can go it alone when we engage the enemy in battle? Do you envision yourself as a kind of spiritual howitzer that can mow down demons and rattle the gates of hell through your own power and poignancy in prayer?

No! Prayer works best in community. Spiritual battle is most effective when you've got an army at your back. So when it comes time to roll up your sleeves and fight for the side of good through prayer, first pick up the phone and call your family. Call your friends. Call your neighbors. Call your church. Call your small group or your life group or whatever they call groups in your congregation.

Join with others in fasting and prayer, as Esther did. And then prepare yourself to see the power of God at work, just as Esther saw.

Ultimately, the queen did stand before the king after three days of fasting and prayer, and she was extended favor once again. I don't have space in these pages to walk through the details of Esther's clever plan to expose Haman's treachery, but it's enough to mention that he was exposed. Not only that, Haman was eventually hanged on the same gallows he had prepared for his enemy, Mordecai.

Justice was served.

Daughters of Justice

The book of Esther could have been a very different story. If Esther had decided to stay on the sidelines and hope for the best on behalf of her people, she would have been just another young woman who won a reality show and lived out the rest of her days in a cocoon of ignorance and wealth. Perhaps *Real House-wives of Persia.*

Thankfully, Esther made the right choice. She jumped into the fight with both fists. And she made a difference not just for her people, but in history.

Thus, Esther's story is ultimately about justice. It's about standing against injustice. It's about resisting hatred and prejudice and the deep-seated antagonisms of our past.

In this way, Esther's story reminds me of another story from the Old Testament—one that is both similar and different in several ways. I'd like to finish out this chapter by quickly exploring the often overlooked tale of Zelophehad's daughters.

When the Israelites were about ready to enter the promised land after wandering in the wilderness for forty years, God gave commands through Moses describing which tribes of Israel would be assigned to different regions to build their new homes. Each of the twelve tribes was allotted a different portion of land, and then the different families within that tribe were each given a section of that allotment.

A man named Zelophehad had died while the Israelites wandered in the wilderness. He had several daughters but no sons and no other male heirs. In the ancient world, daughters did not inherit land or property from their fathers. It was only given to sons. Therefore, tradition dictated that whatever land would have gone to him would be assigned to another family instead.

Zelophehad's daughters were understandably frustrated by this arrangement. Based on the customs of their day, the only way each daughter could be provided for was to find a husband. They were entirely dependent on men to secure their futures.

Incredibly, these particular women not only rejected the status quo, but brought their case before God. Their names were Mahlah, Noah, Hoglah, Milkah, and Tirzah. With great courage and determination, they "stood before Moses, Eleazar the priest, the leaders and the whole assembly at the entrance to the tent of meeting and said, 'Our father died in the wilderness. He was not among Korah's followers, who banded together against the Lord, but he died for his own sin and left no sons. Why should our father's name disappear from his clan because he had no son? Give us property among our father's relatives'" (Num. 27:2–4).

I love the boldness of these women! I admire their fire. They stood before Moses, perhaps the greatest leader in the history of the world outside of Jesus Himself. They stood before the entire collection of authorities and officials in their community. *And they made demands!* "Give us property among our father's relatives."

When Moses went before God to intercede for these daughters, these women, he received an answer. "What Zelophehad's daughters are saying is right," God told him. "You must certainly give them property as an inheritance among their father's relatives and give their father's inheritance to them" (v. 7).

Not only that, but God commanded Moses to change the laws among the Israelites so that any other women who found themselves in the same position as Zelophehad's daughters would be given property of their own. This was a landmark moment for women in the ancient world. This was the equivalent of a Supreme Court case that changed the legal system in a way that created new opportunities for women in their community and beyond.

In short, Mahlah, Noah, Hoglah, Milkah, and Tirzah took a stand against injustice. They argued with passion and purpose for what they believed to be right, and they were vindicated. Better still, the effects of that vindication brought a new ray of light into a dark and dangerous world—a ripple of equality that spread out across centuries.

We need more women like Zelophehad's daughters

in the world today. We need more Esthers. We need women who are willing to stand up for what they believe in not only with words, but with action.

We need women to say "Enough!" when drugs and alcohol ravage their communities. We need women to stand in front of mayors and aldermen and city councils and demand an end to injustice. We need women to *become* mayors and aldermen and city councilors—and governors and senators and, yes, we need women willing to shoulder the burden of the presidency and serve their country as Esther did.

We need strong women in this world—but please hear me say again that strength alone will not win the day. Tenacity alone will not push back the darkness and bring light to a desperate people. Passion alone will not bring an end to tyranny and injustice.

The world needs women who are strong in prayer. The world needs women who are conduits of God's strength and God's tenacity and God's passion.

Because when women pray, they gain victory over injustice.

CHAPTER 8

Rhoda

*When women pray, people are set
free from bondage.*

As Rhoda slipped back into the main room of her
master's house, she once again heard the murmur
of many voices. More than a dozen people were scattered around the room, some kneeling by themselves
on the floor and others huddled in groups of three
or four. Rhoda could sense the tension in the air—a
heaviness pressing down against her spirit.

We are fighting, she thought. *But what if we lose?*

Moving softly, she heard snippets of whispered
prayers as she set food and drink on the low table in
the center of the space: "Lord Jesus, we praise you.

Lord Jesus, we seek your face." "Bind up the work of Satan in Jerusalem. In the name of Jesus we bind up the work of Satan in the prison. In the name of Jesus we bind up the work of Satan in Herod's household." "Your Holy Spirit is with Peter now. Please send your angels, Lord Jesus, to release your servant from bondage."

Some of the guests acknowledged Rhoda as she placed a cup next to them or cleared away a crust of bread. They nodded or smiled—quick gestures. Most simply continued to pray.

Returning to the kitchen with a load of garbage and empty cups, Rhoda recalled how Peter had stood in the main room of the house only a few days before. Always larger than life, Peter had walked endlessly among the brothers and sisters gathered there, his voice booming out with words of encouragement. She remembered the way he grasped the men's shoulders as he spoke. The way he seemed to be always smiling.

He took my hand in his and spoke a blessing over me, she thought. *His hands were so rough and calloused— not like my master's. But his words were gentle and kind.*

She hated the thought of that good and humble man now locked inside a Roman prison. Guards next to him. Chained to him. But even that image paled in comparison to what might happen tomorrow, once the magistrates made their ruling. *They already murdered James*, she thought. *What will happen to us if Peter is next?*

Her work finished for the moment, Rhoda returned to the main room and knelt down outside the ring of visitors. She closed her eyes and tried to let her thoughts drain away. "Lord Jesus, have mercy on me, a sinner," she whispered. "Lord Jesus, have mercy on me, a sinner."

A new sound pricked her ears, and she looked up in surprise. *Was that a knock? No...*

"Lord Jesus, have mercy—" She had just returned to her prayer when the knock came again. Yes, this time it was certainly a knock. The heavy door muffled the noise a bit, but she had answered that door hundreds of times in recent weeks. She knew the sound.

Her first reaction was a quick stab of fear. *Guards sent by Herod!* she thought. *They have come for the rest of us!* But no. That could not be. *Soldiers don't knock on doors*, she reminded herself. *Soldiers break them down.*

Standing, her heart still pounding, she made her way toward the door even as she heard the knock a third time.

Who on earth could it be?

Ordinary People

I want to talk about this woman named Rhoda because it's possible you've never heard of her. But first I need to explain what was happening in Acts 12, which is where we find her in Scripture.

The earliest days of the church were turbulent in many ways. After the events surrounding the crucifixion, the religious leaders in Jerusalem believed they had solved their "Jesus problem." *We have struck the shepherd,* they reasoned, *and the sheep are certain to scatter.*

That didn't happen. Instead, the sheep—the earliest followers of Jesus—began telling everyone who would listen that Jesus was alive. He had risen from the dead. Then the sheep began performing miracles. The same kinds of miracles Jesus Himself had performed. All of a sudden there were more and more sheep everywhere you looked. Sometimes thousands of people were added to the church in a single day. The movement was growing exponentially.

At first, the religious leaders in Jerusalem tried to respond cautiously. In Acts 4, for example, they arrested Peter and John for preaching about Jesus, but they issued a warning. The members of the Sanhedrin commanded Peter and John "not to speak or teach at all in the name of Jesus" (v. 18). This was a slap on the wrist. They were playing nice.

To Peter and John's credit, they didn't play along. "Which is right in God's eyes: to listen to you, or to him? You be the judges!" they said. "As for us, we cannot help speaking about what we have seen and heard" (vv. 19–20).

Later, when the church continued to grow, the religious leaders in Jerusalem got serious. They arrested more of these "Christians"—followers of the way. They locked entire families in jail and kept them there. Then, as described in Acts 7, they arrested a young man named Stephen and charged him with speaking blasphemy against God. Instead of jail, they stoned Stephen to death. No more playing nice. It was time to nip this movement in the bud.

Scripture says, "On that day a great persecution broke out against the church in Jerusalem, and all except the apostles were scattered throughout Judea and Samaria" (Acts 8:1). Ironically, this persecution actually fueled the expansion of the church to a whole new level. As people fled Jerusalem to escape the wrath of the Jewish leaders, they took the gospel with them. And the movement continued to spread.

Around that same time, a man named Saul "began

to destroy the church. Going from house to house, he dragged off both men and women and put them in prison" (8:3). This Saul later became known as Paul. After his own encounter with the risen Christ, Paul was transformed into the greatest missionary this world has ever known.

In Acts 12 we see King Herod get involved in the persecution of Christians. He carried the authority of Rome in his pocket, which made him a dangerous foe. Herod ordered the arrest and execution of James, the brother of the apostle John and one of the "sons of thunder." When he saw how happy that decision made the religious leaders of Jerusalem, he also sent word for Peter to be arrested.

That's where Rhoda entered the picture. After Peter's arrest, the leaders of the church in Jerusalem gathered together to pray. They stayed together for hours, pouring out their hearts before God and asking that Peter's life would be spared. Rhoda was inside that house, but she wasn't one of the leaders. She wasn't one of the wealthier folks who had church services in her home. She wasn't even married to one of the church leaders.

No, Rhoda was a servant. She was staff. An employee. The text simply describes her as "a servant named Rhoda" (Acts 12:13).

One of the things I love most about the Bible is the

way it consistently and unashamedly elevates the status of regular people. Rhoda was a servant, yet as we'll soon see, she took part in a miracle. Most of Jesus' disciples were fishermen, which means they were largely uneducated. They weren't good enough in Hebrew school to become scribes or rabbis.

Joshua was a soldier. Rahab was a prostitute, and Ruth gleaned food from other people's fields after they'd been harvested, which means she was almost a beggar. Yet both of those women are listed in the Scripture as ancestors of Jesus. David started out as a shepherd. Elisha was a farmer before he took on Elijah's mantle. Joseph was a carpenter. One of Jesus' apostles was called "Simon the Zealot," which means he was a rabble rouser; today we might call him a terrorist.

Even Peter is a great example. He was another fisherman, and he was the kind of guy who never seemed able to keep his foot outside of his mouth. He was coarse. He cussed. He boasted and tried to make himself look better than others. One time he even got on Jesus' case so bad, Jesus had to rebuke him by saying, "Get behind me, Satan!" (Mark 8:33).

In spite of all that, Peter was *the* face of the early church. We recognize Paul as a great man now because he wrote so much of the New Testament, but we don't always realize that Peter was the one out in front before the church was even a church. Peter was the one preaching the sermon on the Day of Pentecost. Peter was walked the streets performing miracles and stirring up trouble to the point where he got himself arrested, all in the name of Jesus and for His glory.

God loves regular people—the kinds of people who are typically pushed behind the scenes of society. People like Rhoda. God not only loves such people, but He understands their value. He understands their uniqueness and their unique contributions to this world.

If the Bible were written today, it would be filled with Uber drivers and kindergarten teachers. We would read verses about plumbers performing miracles and custodians casting out demons. The Holy Spirit would reveal the gospel through the fingers and the lips of immigrants and grocery clerks and baristas and factory workers.

Because God understand the value of ordinary people. People like Rhoda.

Extraordinary Power

Taking it even further, not only does the Bible lift up the value of ordinary people, but the Bible highlights exactly what can happen when ordinary people pray, people like Rhoda and those who were with her when Peter was in prison.

Because when ordinary people pray, they gain access to extraordinary power.

Look at what the text says: "The night before Herod was to bring him to trial, Peter was sleeping between two soldiers, bound with two chains, and sentries stood guard at the entrance" (Acts 12:6).

Now, that's a serious situation. Not only was Peter in a jail cell, but there were two soldiers in there with him. And not only were the soldiers in the cell with Peter, but they had him surrounded. He had to sleep between them; he couldn't even get a corner over there by himself for a little privacy. And not only did Peter have to sleep between two soldiers, but he was bound with chains—and those chains were probably connected to those very same soldiers. And not only was Peter chained to the soldiers who were surrounding him in a jail cell, but there were two more soldiers outside the cell keeping watch just in case Peter somehow managed to slip the chains and make a break for the door.

Do you know what I call that kind of situation? Bondage. Peter was in bondage.

Whenever I think about prisons or jails, I am hit

with vivid visions of my experiences at Elmina Castle in Ghana. If you're not familiar with that name, it's the place where slaves were kept in cells before being shipped out to America or other ports around the world.

I can remember placing my own fingers on the grooves and scratch marks that score the interior of the castle walls. Those grooves were caused by slaves trying to claw their way through the stone with nothing but their fingernails in their desperation to escape—in their desperation to be set free. I can also remember the building just across the way from the castle where the slave owners gathered for church each week. They worshiped God even as they made plans to shackle His people and separate families and sell what God alone had purchased through the sacrifice of His Son.

What I learned there at the castle is that the prayer for freedom is often born out of adversity. It's born out of terror. Many times our prayers begin when the medicine ends.

Of course, bondage is still a fact of life today, including physical bondage. There are still followers of Jesus all over the world who wake up and go to sleep in a concrete cell. Some of them are incarcerated because of their belief in Christ—religious persecution remains a reality. Others are incarcerated as a consequence of wrong choices. Yet others are incarcerated because broken systems create broken people, and because injustice creates oppression.

Between 1980 and 2015 in the United States of America, my country, the number of incarcerated individuals increased from 500,000 to more than 2.2 million. A majority of those prisoners have been African American men. In fact, black men are incarcerated more than five times as frequently as white men; similarly, black women are twice as likely to be jailed as white women.[1]

The effects of this imbalance in my community cannot be overstated. Generations of black children have grown up fatherless because their fathers are locked away. And when black men are given back their freedom, they often find it nearly impossible to find gainful employment because of the stain of incarceration. Families are suffering, and many in our community distrust the very authorities who are charged with our protection.

That is bondage. That is a system of bondage.

But the reality of bondage carries much further than courthouses and jails. There are more kinds of bars in this world than prison bars.

There's relational bondage, for example, where the very walls of your home feel like prison walls. You live in fear of what might happen if your spouse gets angry or something triggers an outbreak of rage. You're not safe. You're not protected. Yet you don't see any way to get out in one piece.

There's financial bondage, in which your lack of resources is like a tether staking you to the ground. You have hopes and dreams. You have ambitions. You want to stretch your wings and fly, but you cannot because there are no resources to launch you forward. You're stuck. Locked down by everything you lack.

Then there's the bondage of dependency. Addiction is a serious shackle, no matter what the source of that addiction might be. Drugs. Alcohol. Pornography. Relational codependency. Often your own body turns against you to the point where it seems even the ability to choose has been removed.

Let me ask you, then, in what ways are you currently living in bondage? When you lie down to sleep each night, who are the soldiers that press close? When did you first feel the cold harshness of the chains against your wrists, and what were those chains made from?

Here's a principle I hope you hear and understand: if you feel locked down and chained up, and you're beginning to lose any hope of freedom—that is a time to pray, because ordinary prayers have extraordinary power to free you from your bondage.

That's what Peter experienced. According to the text, "Suddenly an angel of the Lord appeared and a light shone in the cell. He struck Peter on the side and woke him up. 'Quick, get up!' he said, and the chains fell off Peter's wrists" (Acts 12:7). The angel led Peter past the outer guards and up into the open air, opening doors and unlocking locks where necessary.

The funny thing about this entire situation is that Peter had no idea it was real. The text says, "he thought he was seeing a vision" (v. 9). That's a nice way of saying Peter thought it was all a dream—a pleasant fantasy while in reality he was still snoozing away between the soldiers. When it finally kicked in that he really had been rescued, Peter said, "Now I know without a doubt that the Lord has sent his angel and rescued me from Herod's clutches" (v. 11).

That's freedom. And that is the kind of extraordinary power we can access as a community when ordinary people pray.

Open the Door

There's an interesting dynamic I want to highlight in how all this worked out. Specifically, there are two locations at play—two settings in the story.

First was the house where the different leaders of the church had gathered to pray for Peter. The house where Rhoda was a servant. Can you picture them in their prayers? Men and women of different ages, all crying out together on Peter's behalf. Imagine what it must have sounded like. Imagine the spiritual energy in that room—the earnestness and the expectation.

Second was the prison on the other side of town. The one where Peter had been chained up and locked in—for a time.

What I want you to see is that while the group in that house was praying in one part of the city, God was *simultaneously* at work in the prison across town. We know God was at work in one sense because the text says, "Peter was sleeping between two soldiers" (v. 6). The only way you can sleep when you're crammed between two soldiers and you expect to be put to death in the morning is that God is with you and has brought you His peace. His comfort. His supernatural gift of rest.

More than that, as the people in the house continued to pray—with great fervency and great faith, I'm sure—God sent His angel to break Peter out of the prison. While the people were still in the middle of their prayers, God had already moved to answer them with supernatural power.

Here's my point: when you choose to engage with God in prayer, there comes a point early in that process when you need to trust that He is on the case—even if you don't see any evidence of an answer. Perhaps *especially* when you see no evidence of an answer.

I remember when I traveled to Charlotte to visit my mother, who was in the hospital. I was on my way up to see her when somebody recognized me in the hallway. "Bishop Jakes!" she said, "I've seen you on television! This has to be a sign from God. My mother is brain dead—she can't sit up or speak. The doctors say there is no hope. Will you come pray for her?"

What I wanted to say in that moment was something like this: "I'll have someone send you a tape to play, but right now I'm on the way to see my own momma."

What I actually said was, "Where is she?"

And even though I didn't feel it, even though I wasn't excited about it, I followed that woman down the hall and prayed for her mother. And as I prayed, I felt the presence of God in that room. There was no evidence from the mother—she didn't squeeze my hand or groan or grunt. But I was aware of God's Spirit.

When the prayer was over, I went on and attended to my own mother. I never expected to see that other woman again, but about a year later I was leading one of our Woman Thou Art Loosed gatherings in the same city, and here she came walking through the door. She was using a cane, but she was walking. And she said to me, "Pastor Jakes, you probably don't remember, but my daughter said you prayed for me. And the next morning I woke from that coma, and the doctors said it was a miracle."

What I learned in that moment is that you never know what God will do in response to the prayers of His people. There is extraordinary power when ordinary people pray—people like you and me.

I know there are times when it feels like your prayers have no effect. I know there are moments when it seems like everything you say, everything you pray, is bouncing off the ceiling and falling right back down around your feet.

What I need you to understand is that God is up to something. Even when you can't see what's going on, He's up to something. Even when you don't feel His presence or His power, He's up to something. Even when you've been praying for months or years or even decades and nothing has happened and you are bogged down by doubt and desperation—that is a time to trust Him and keep on praying, because He's up to something.

Peter found out what God was up to. So did Rhoda. She was in with all the church leaders, praying for God to work a miracle. And even though God *did* work that miracle, He didn't send a memo into that room. He didn't give them a status update where He said, "Attention, your prayers are being answered, please stand by."

No, what happened is Rhoda heard a knock on the door.

The text says, "Peter knocked at the outer entrance, and a servant named Rhoda came to answer the door. When she recognized Peter's voice, she was so overjoyed she ran back without opening it and exclaimed, 'Peter is at the door!'" (Acts 12:13–14).

It wasn't the owner of the house who heard the evidence of God's answer to their prayers. It wasn't any of the church leaders down on their knees and pouring out their voices. No, it was Rhoda who heard the knocking, and it was Rhoda who went to answer.

Just one thing, though: she forgot to open the door.

This may sound strange, but oftentimes the devil doesn't really mind it when Christians do what we do. He doesn't mind when preachers preach about transformation and restoration and healing and all that. He doesn't get worried when we gather together and sing our songs or dance in the aisles or even when we pray in tongues. He's not afraid of our small groups and our Sunday school classes and our service projects.

In short, Satan is okay with church people doing church things—as long as we don't open the door.

What do I mean by that? I mean it's common for God's people to get caught up in the rituals and the trappings of looking like God's people without actually taking hold of God's power. And that is what the devil fears: God's power at work in our lives. God's power set loose in the world.

Rhoda heard Peter's knocking and she recognized Peter's voice. But she forgot to open the door.

There comes a time in the practice of prayer when we need to recognize what God is doing around us. We need to hear the knocking at the door. When that moment comes, we need to switch gears. We need to take off our mourning clothes and put an end to our weeping and feeling sorry for ourselves—because that which we have been praying for is standing at the door!

At some point your prayers will accomplish all they were designed to do, and it will be time for you to act. Do you remember when Jesus healed the paralyzed man after his friends lowered him through a hole in the ceiling? Jesus told him his sins were forgiven. But then Jesus said, "Get up, take your mat and go home" (Luke 5:24).

Just like that man's friends, Rhoda had the faith necessary to pray for Peter's release. She had faith to believe God *could* do something big, and she had the presence of mind to hear the knocking once God *did* do something big. She had faith to get up and go to the door. She had enough faith to test the provision that had been sent her way; she recognized Peter's voice. She even had enough faith to resist the others in the house when they told her she was crazy or that she must have encountered Peter's ghost.

But she forgot to open the door.

I want to see a new generation of women rising up in the same spirit as Rhoda—ordinary women who possess Rhoda's faith. But just as important, I am serving notice on Satan that this new generation will not stop at the door, as Rhoda did. No, this new generation of women who pray will open the door of God's extraordinary power. And if the door gets stuck a little bit, this new generation of women who pray will be ready to kick it down!

That's what we need in the world today. That's what will release God's power in your life and in the lives of those you love. That's what will break the chains that are holding us down. God's extraordinary power will flow through the prayers of ordinary people when we have the faith to pray—and when we are willing to take action to open the door and take hold of what God has set before us.

I'm tired of all the arguing about denominations and doctrines. I'm tired of all the squabbles about which church is best and what kind of worship is best and whether we can accommodate black folks and white folks and brown folks in the same building. I'm tired of the church sitting comfortably in its chains and lacking any motivation to bust out of the prison of ineffectiveness.

I want to see ordinary women who are ready to embrace extraordinary lives built on prayer. Because when women pray, people are set free from bondage.

CHAPTER 9

The Shunammite Woman

*When women pray, even what is
dead can find life again.*

She was already waiting in the street when her husband left the house. He adjusted his tunic as he walked by, his belly full once more from the morning meal.

"Why do you strain your eyes in search of this man?" he asked. "If he comes today, he comes. If not today, he will come another. Go inside and keep the sun off your face."

"Yes, my husband," she answered. She watched from the doorway as he began his long, lumbering journey toward the fields.

He will come today, she thought. *He has passed through our town on the same day for five weeks now. He will do so again today.*

Of course everyone in Shunem had heard about this prophet named Elijah. This man of God. Stories were told about him from Jerusalem to Damascus and well beyond. *But I have seen him,* she thought. *I have spoken with him many times. And after today, perhaps he will count me among his friends, though I am not one of his people.*

She remembered her first encounter with the man of God. When she saw him stopped in the street, speaking with his servant, she had offered food and drink. At the time, it was nothing more than her custom. She was a woman of hospitality and her husband a man of means. She gave for the joy of giving.

While speaking with this man, however, she had recognized the difference in him. The strangeness about him. He carried an authority she could not deny. A power she had not witnessed or perceived even among the most holy of her people's priests.

He is a man of God in truth, she had thought. *He gives me hope that such a thing as God may actually be real.*

From that point on, she had remained watchful. Waiting. Every time she saw Elijah and his servant walking up the street, she was ready with a meal. Something hot to drink. A place to rest after a weary walk.

Now she had something more to offer. It had taken much convincing, but her husband had finally given permission for one of his servants to add a room at the top of their house. Nothing fancy; she knew a true man of God would be skeptical of luxury. But she felt sure he would welcome a place to rest. He and his servant.

Just a room, a bed, a chair, and a lamp, she thought. *A table, too.*

She saw a stirring of dust out along the distant stretch of road. Was that the silhouette of one man or two? It looked like two.

Stepping back into the house, she called her servants to begin preparations. Just some food and drink. Just a room and a chair.

He may accept, she thought. *And perhaps our home will again be blessed because of his presence.*

Space for God

We come now to another woman whose name is not recorded in Scripture. Scholars and Bible teachers typically refer to her as "the Shunammite woman." She has been defined for millennia by nothing more significant than her hometown.

When we look more closely at the text, however, we can see right away that this was not your average woman.

The text describes her as "a well-to-do woman," meaning she had money. Or perhaps more likely, her husband had money. The old King James translation describes her as "a great woman." I like that better.

Moreover, this was a woman of great hospitality. Now, you may know that hospitality was a critical virtue in the ancient world, and it is still a prized priority in the Middle East. But as you'll see, this woman went above and beyond. The text says Elijah the prophet was on a journey through Shunem, her home town, and she "urged" him to stay for a meal. She didn't "consent." She didn't "concede." She didn't act in response to Elijah's request. Instead, she saw that Elijah and his servant were hungry and she proactively and with great generosity "urged" that she be allowed to meet their need.

I have known many great women over the course of my lifetime. And when I say "great," I don't necessarily mean "famous." I've had wonderful interactions with Oprah Winfrey, Coretta Scott King, and other women who are both great and famous. But there are many, many women in the world today who are both great and unknown. Unheralded.

My mother and grandmother were great women, for example. My wife and her mother are great women. There are great women who attend our church every week. There are great women who give of their own resources to bless others through our Woman Thou Art Loosed gatherings. There are great women in families and communities all across the world who are wise in their counsel, generous in their hospitality, and strong in their spiritual connection to God.

Here's something I can say with complete confidence: Every time I've had the privilege to interact with a great woman, I have come away blessed. I have come away filled. I have come away rejuvenated and restored.

Great women are an incredible asset in this world. And in my observation, great women are almost always women of prayer.

The Shunammite woman was a great woman, and she had the wisdom to recognize the uniqueness of Elijah. Specifically, she recognized Elijah's connection to God. Elijah himself was not a great man, but he had a powerful connection to a great God. Therefore, this woman built a room for Elijah and his servant to use whenever they passed through the town of Shunem. She built a place for them to stay where they would have some measure of comfort and security.

In other words, the Shunammite woman made space for Elijah in her home. And in doing so, she made space for the work of God in her life.

I love the picture there because it illustrates an important truth: If you want to see God work in your life, you need to make space for Him. If you want to experience God's presence and power, you need to give Him some room to move. Room to breathe.

In the same way, if you want to experience God's blessings—if you want Him to fill you up with what you need and what you desire—you need to make some space. You need to open up an area in which you can receive what you need and what you desire.

Have you noticed how busy people are in today's world? Especially women. Sometimes there is simply no room for anything else to happen. When you fill your day with work and you're making calls even during your commute, you leave no space for God. When you've got so many hobbies and projects that you can't even keep track of what's going on, you leave no space for God. When you give everything you have to your family because you're desperate for their approval, you leave no space for God. And when you line up a whole season of TV shows on your DVR and just binge watch episode after episode, you leave no space for God.

God is not a divine vacuum salesman who will try to force His way into your house or your life. He will wait until you offer Him some space to work, and then He will work.

Make space for God in your life. Otherwise, you will have no room for prayer.

Needs and Desires

After being on the receiving end of this woman's generosity, Elijah had his servant call to her and ask, "You have gone to all this trouble for us. Now what can be done for you? Can we speak on your behalf to the king or the commander of the army?" (2 Kings 4:13). Elijah wanted to repay her kindness with kindness.

The text says she replied, "I have a home among my own people" (v. 13). In other words, "I'm good. I've got everything I need."

Elijah kept digging. He spoke with his servant,. Gehazi, to try to get his opinion on some way they could repay the kindness of this woman. And Gehazi said, "She has no son, and her husband is old" (v. 14).

What a description. What a summation of this woman's circumstances. We saw in the chapter about Sarah the way childlessness was a terrible stigma in the ancient world. And to make matters worse, this woman's husband was old. Meaning, she had no hope of improving her situation.

The prophet called out to the Shunammite woman again and said, "About this time next year, you will hold a son in your arms" (v. 16).

Look at how she responded: "No, my lord!" she objected. "Please, man of God, don't mislead your servant!" (v. 16).

Why would this woman recoil so forcefully against the promise of a son? Because she had buried her hope so deeply that it hurt to start digging it up again. This woman had pressed down her desire for children over the course of years. She felt that desire—she longed for the feeling of a baby in her arms and the sound of a child's laughter in her home. But she had smothered those desires.

This woman had a hole in her heart, but she had stuffed that hole full of money and possessions and comfort in an attempt to snuff out her desire for children. She had smothered that desire and pushed it down deeper and deeper until she convinced herself it was dead.

But that's one of the dangers of making space for God in your life, because He has a way of putting His finger on what we long for most. That's one of the dangers of making space for prayer in our lives—because prayer can bring life to that which we believed to be dead.

How often do we try to convince ourselves we don't need anything? How often do we try to convince others that we have it all together? How often do we try to convince God? We feel the movement of His Spirit as He reaches out to offer a blessing, but we shake our heads. "I'm good. I've got everything I need."

Here's a principle: No matter how hard you try, you can't hide your desires from God. No matter how stridently you deny your own heart, you can't hide your longings from God. He knows. And He will put His finger on those desires when you give Him room to do so through prayer.

The reality is that human beings are highly adaptable creatures. As we make our way from point to point in our lives, we often have to adapt to changing situations. We have to get used to new feelings and new circumstances. We have to learn to operate in new conditions around new people—otherwise we won't survive.

This is a good thing, for the most part. It's a good

thing when people are able to adapt to change and continue to thrive, because if we know anything about life, it's that change is inevitable.

The problem comes when our adaptation leads to acceptance of something we should never accept. This almost always happens because of trials and tragedy. When we are forced to endure difficult circumstances, we adapt to those circumstances by finding ways to minimize the pain we experience. We learn how to short-circuit our own suffering so that we can survive the situation and move forward.

The Shunammite woman had adapted to her situation by accepting her barrenness. And so she was shocked and perhaps even appalled when Elijah poked at her wound.

What have you accepted in your life that should have no place in your life? What have you accepted into your family that should have no place in your family?

Have you accepted spiritual barrenness? Have you accepted brokenness, either in yourself or in your children? In your spouse? Have you accepted burdens you were never meant to carry? Have you accepted relationships that are dragging you down? Have you accepted abuse or unhappiness or disrespect?

One of the reasons you try to deny your longings

and your desires is because you've been stung so many times by disappointment. You used to hold out hope; you used to believe and yearn and pray for God to provide that which you desired most to hold. But it never came. The prayers were never answered. And so in order to protect yourself from any further stings— in order to protect yourself from disappointment—you allowed a crust to form over your heart. A hardness. A callousness. A defense mechanism.

Thankfully, God has a way of breaking through that crust. He has a way of breaching our defenses and touching our hearts when He knows the timing is right.

That's exactly what God did for the Shunammite woman.

The Death of Her Dream

Scripture is very matter-of-fact about this miracle in the life of the Shunammite woman: "But the woman became pregnant, and the next year about that same time she gave birth to a son, just as Elisha had told her" (v. 17). Problem solved.

But stop for a moment and try to imagine the joy this woman must have felt. The incredible, life-giving, hope-sustaining joy. Can you see her nursing the child by that same window she used to look through when she was waiting for Elijah to pass by? Can you see her carrying the boy up to Elijah's room and letting him play on the bed when the prophet was away? Can you hear her words as she introduced the child to her neighbors and friends? "Yes, I knew it would be a boy because of the prophet's promise."

I love it when great women are given great gifts. So many women are used to pouring out all the time. They pour out their time for others. They pour out their talents for others. They pour out their energy and their strength and sometimes even their sanity as they perform task after task, project after project in service to those they love.

It's wonderful when those women have a moment of being *poured in* rather than *poured out*.

How tragic, then, when we read what happened next:

> The child grew, and one day he went out to his father, who was with the reapers. He said to his father, "My head! My head!"
>
> His father told a servant, "Carry him to his mother." After the servant had lifted him up and carried him to his mother, the boy sat

on her lap until noon, and then he died. She
went up and laid him on the bed of the man
of God, then shut the door and went out.
(vv. 18–21)

Our immediate reaction to these verses is, *How?
Why?* After everything this woman had experienced,
after she finally received the desire of her heart—why
would God step in and pluck the child away? How
could that happen?

Now, I don't want to get carried away down a rabbit
hole, but I need to pause for just a moment and take
a look at the stupidity of the Shunammite woman's
husband. This is the kind of man that really gets my
hackles up.

For one thing, the boy is there in the field, screaming, "My head! My head!" You probably understand
that heads are important. The boy's mother understood heads are important. The servants there in the
field understood it. But the father was clueless. He told
one of the servants, "Carry him to his mother." The
man did not have the empathy or emotional urgency
to even carry his own son to safety. He turned the boy
over to one of the servants and kept working.

Later that day, after the boy had died, the Shunammite woman called out to her husband and asked for a

donkey so she could "quickly" reach the man of God. "Why go to him today?" he asked. "It's not the New Moon or the Sabbath" (v. 23).

Not that long ago, this man's son was carried to his mother, screaming in pain, because something was wrong with his head. Then the mother comes rushing out of the house and says, "I have to see the preacher quick. Get me a donkey so I can get on my way." Any intelligent person should be able to make a connection between those two events. Any father who cares about his family should have realized something might be wrong with his son. At the very least, a husband who knows anything about his wife should be able to recognize in her face that she is responding to something very serious and that she is terrified.

But no. This fool asked, "Why do you need to see the preacher? It's not Sunday." The man never stopped his work. The man never asked what was wrong. The man wasn't even aware his own son had died.

There's a saying that behind every great man stands a great woman, but I'm sorry to say the opposite is not always true. There are many great women in the world today who suffer under the leadership of brutes. There are many wonderful daughters who are stunted in their growth and their outlook on life because they're stuck with deadbeat dads.

In short, there are a lot of great women today who are married to great fools who are supposed to be men. The plain truth is that husbands can let you down. Your extended family can let you down. Even the systems in our churches and our communities and our nations can let you down and try to keep you down.

All of which are critical reasons why women need to pray.

That's what the Shunammite woman did. Her dream had died in her arms. The son she longed to hold for so many years—the son that was promised and delivered by God—had been taken away. And she was desperate. She did the only thing she could think to do, which was run to the man of God.

When she reached Elijah, the text says she "took hold of his feet" (v. 27). She latched on. She grabbed hold of the only power she hoped would be strong enough to do something about her situation.

Oh, that you might be like this woman when tragedy strikes your home! Oh, that you might respond the way this woman responded when despair and hopelessness threaten your family.

How often do we respond to tragedy with stoicism? How often do we try to pretend like everything is all right? How often do we try to convince ourselves we don't really need that thing we lost—that person or that dream or that vision or that truth—simply because we lost it? That is the easy path. That is the coward's way out. To pretend something doesn't hurt us when everyone can see we are devastated and distraught.

The Shunammite woman made the right choice because she ran toward God—she ran toward His prophet. And when she got within sight of Elijah, she dived onto the ground and took hold of his feet. Not only that, she told Elijah, "As surely as the Lord lives and as you live, I will not leave you" (v. 30).

In other words, this woman was not letting go of God's prophet until God unleashed His power to solve her problem.

That is a picture of prayer. Don't deny your needs. Don't deny the pain you feel. Run to God! Grab hold of Him and refuse to let go! Because He is able to bring your dreams to life, even when it sure looks to you and everyone else like they died long ago.

To finish the story, Elijah rushed back with the woman and went up to the room to see her son. He stretched out over the boy—the text says, "mouth to mouth, eyes to eyes, hands to hands" (v. 33). And the boy's body transformed from the coldness of death to the warmth of life. Scripture says, "The boy sneezed seven times and opened his eyes" (v. 35).

Then Elijah called the woman back into the room and presented her living, breathing, laughing, sneezing son. Her dream was alive once more. Why? Because of prayer. Because she refused to accept her situation as it was and instead chose to run after God's prophet and God's power.

I hope you'll make the same choice when it feels like your dreams are dying—when it seems like hope itself is slipping through your fingers. I hope you'll run to God and dive at His feet. I hope you'll grab Him and refuse to let go.

Because when women pray, even what is dead can find life again.

CHAPTER 10

Anna

When women pray, people find salvation.

Anna felt a tickle on the back of her neck. A tingle that was both strange and familiar. Looking up, she thought a breath of wind must have swept through the temple courtyards, but then she realized she was still wearing her shawl. Her skin was covered.

Perhaps a different kind of wind, she thought. *Perhaps another type of breath.*

She reached for her cane and then—slowly, carefully, being certain of each movement—rose to her feet. Her knees popped as she straightened. Her back creaked. She had been praying for several hours, and she knew from experience it would be some minutes before she could walk.

One day I will be unable to rise, she mused. *I will simply settle to the ground and stay there until someone finds the body.*

The thought did not trouble her. She was eighty-four years old, and she had spent more than sixty years living and worshiping in the temple. Certainly she expected to die here.

When the painful prickling up and down her legs began to subside, Anna took a few cautious steps forward. Everything seemed to be working. She changed direction and began moving toward her small quarters built against the outer wall of the temple.

For some reason, Anna's thoughts returned to her husband as she walked. She'd been thinking about him more often in recent weeks, though she hadn't seen his face for more than sixty years.

What would he say if he saw me shuffling and shambling around like this? she wondered. The answer came almost immediately. *He would say it's ironic that the girl who always dreamed of traveling to distant cities has spent her entire life in the same courtyard doing the same thing day after day.*

She chuckled at the thought. Her husband did have a good sense of humor.

There were always many people moving about the temple courtyards, and many voices calling and shouting to one another. She usually ignored them, though her hearing was still sharp as ever. Today, though, she turned her head at the sound of Simeon's voice. Another old soldier, like herself. Another who spent his life waiting to see what everyone hoped to see but almost no one believed would actually appear.

"For my eyes have seen your salvation," Simeon was saying. He held a baby in his arms—very young, with both parents standing close. Protective. "A light for revelation to the Gentiles, and the glory of your people."

Could it be? Anna wondered. She quickened her pace as the young mother took the baby from Simeon's arms. She was smiling. A lovely girl. So young.

But Anna had eyes only for the child.

Yes, she thought. *My Lord and my God, after all these years—yes.*

Slaves and Saviors

Anna is an interesting character in the Scriptures for several reasons. For one thing, she was eighty-four years old during a period in history when the average life expectancy may have been forty or fifty years. Also, the text says Anna was married to her husband for "seven years" before he died. Then, after his death, she spent the rest of her life—which was likely more than sixty years—praying and worshiping God at the temple. Literally. The text says, "She never left the temple but worshiped night and day, fasting and praying" (Luke 2:37).

Now, I love what we've built at the Potter's House in Dallas. I enjoy spending time there throughout the week, and I especially savor every Sunday service with our church community. But there are still some times when I need to get back to my own house, in my own room, sit down on my own chair, and relax a little bit with some brisket and a good book. I need some me time.

Not Anna. She likely had a small living quarters set up on the temple grounds, and that's where she stayed. Her life was completely devoted to worship, fasting, and praying.

What is most interesting about Anna, however, is her title. Scripture says, "There was also a prophet, Anna, the daughter of Penuel, of the tribe of Asher" (v. 36). Anna was a prophet. She was one of those unique individuals of her generation who heard the voice of God in a powerful way and was charged with communicating His words to the Jewish people and beyond.

It might surprise you to learn that Anna was not the only female prophet in the Bible. In fact, there were several others. Miriam, who was the sister of Moses, was the first woman given that title (see Exod. 15:20). Deborah was one of the "judges" who led the Israelites before the establishment of the monarchy under King Saul; she was also described as "a prophetess" (Judg. 4:4). Huldah was a prophetess who ministered during the reign of Israel's kings (see 2 Chron. 34:22). Isaiah the prophet married a prophetess (Isa. 8:3). And in the New Testament, Philip the evangelist had four unmarried daughters, and the text says they all "prophesied" (Acts 21:9).

The point is that women have access to Almighty God on a direct line, just as men do. Yes, there are biblical roles established in the household for husbands and wives. And yes, there are instructions given in the New Testament for how to structure authority and teaching within the church. But on a personal level, there is no requirement for a woman to go through a man in order to connect with God. Women can pick up that big red phone and have instant access to the King.

That leads to an important question: What are you

doing with that access? How often do you pick up that big red phone? Because remember, your direct line to God will only benefit you as much as you use it. That's why I will continue to call for women everywhere to pray.

Now, Anna's status as a prophet likely means she was educated in the Old Testament scriptures. Perhaps that's why the text emphasizes her father, Penuel. You see, most women in the ancient world were forbidden from learning much in terms of school. They were typically forbidden from learning to read and write, and they were usually denied access to the study of God's Word.

I wonder, then, whether Penuel was a bit of a maverick. I wonder if he went out on a limb and decided his daughter needed to understand the Scriptures. If so, Penuel would have taught her about the Jewish patriarchs: Abraham, Isaac, and Jacob. He would have taught her about other key figures such as David and Solomon, Elijah and Elisha, Daniel and Ezekiel.

Certainly, Penuel would have taught his daughter about Moses. He would have walked her through the book of Exodus and described the enslavement of the Israelites during their time in Egypt. He would have narrated the story of Moses' first attempt to rescue his people, when he killed the Egyptian guard and wound up being chased all the way to Midian, where he lived as a shepherd in disgrace for forty years. I can imagine Penuel painting vivid pictures of the burning bush and God's call for Moses to return to Egypt. I can almost see the fear in Anna's eyes and hear her hushed whispers as Penuel described each of the ten plagues in detail, culminating in the death of Pharaoh's own son. I imagine she ducked her head under a blanket in fear when her daddy told her of Pharaoh's army pursuing the Israelites to the border of the Red Sea, and I imagine her bursting back out with a smile when he delivered the triumphant news of God delivering their people by parting the waters at Moses' command and allowing them to walk through the danger of the waters on dry land.

Why am I making such a big deal about Moses here? Because if Anna understood the way her people, the Israelites, were rescued from slavery in Egypt, then she would have recognized a similar slavery during her own time.

The Jewish people of Anna's day weren't back in Egypt, but they had essentially been sold into slavery while they dwelled in their own land. They had been conquered by the Roman Empire. The citizens of Jerusalem and the surrounding villages were vassals of Rome. God's chosen people were forced to pay taxes to foreign rulers and pay homage to foreign gods.

In other words, Anna would have recognized that

her people were once again in need of a Moses—they were once again in need of a savior. And as she lived and worshiped and prayed in the temple day after day, year after year, Anna believed that savior would be arriving soon.

Did you know slavery is still a major factor in the world today? Advocates estimate there are about 40 million people enslaved around the world right now. Today. That's more than the populations of greater New York City and Los Angeles *combined*. About half of that 40 million are people and families locked into "labor slavery," which is when slaves owe debts to their "employers" that are impossible to pay—the people keep working day after day in filthy factories and squalid conditions, but they earn less money than it costs to live. Their debt increases the more they work.

Sex trafficking and sex slavery are another major portion of those 40 million modern slaves. In fact, women and girls make up 71 percent of all the people still enslaved in the modern world.[1]

That's another reason for women to pray.

But there are other kinds of slavery beyond the physical. You can become enslaved by addiction, for example. What started out as something fun or a way to blow off steam can quickly become deadly serious.

When you have become chained by your own choices and you no longer feel in control of your life, you better turn to prayer.

You can be enslaved by injustice. You and your spouse work hard every day to try to make a life for your family. You save resources when you are able, but there never seems to be enough to go around. You've talked endlessly about different options for escape, for moving up and moving out, but the options never become opportunities. You are shackled by a system that keeps you down.

You can also become enslaved by your desires—your wants and wishes. You feel good when you buy yourself something new. Something nice. Maybe you got an ego boost when your outfit looked so much better than those of your coworkers. You felt a thrill when your neighbor saw that new car in your driveway. But the good vibes never last long. They never satisfy, and they always leave you wanting that next item. That next fix. You are bound by your attempts to buy your way into a life of fulfillment.

Here's a principle I hope you'll remember: when you are a slave to something more powerful than yourself, you have no hope of escape through your own power. You need a savior.

A Prayer for Salvation

There's a lot we can admire about Anna. Even though we only can only read about her in two or three verses from the Bible, there's a lot about her life that we can imitate in our own lives.

For example, notice the *persistence* of Anna's prayers. She was dedicated to prayer as the major element of her life. For so many of us, prayer is something we do when we can fit it in. When we can find a little time. Meaning, we have our key priorities over here on one side, and they pretty much determine how we approach our day, our week, our month, and so on. Then, as much as we're able, we fit in some of the other ideas or ideals we think are also important—including prayer.

That's not how Anna approached life. She never left the temple, because prayer *was* her life. It was her priority. Prayer was the foundation around which she built everything else in her day, her week, her month, and so on.

Also notice the *diversity* of Anna's prayer life. It's easy to get stuck in ruts in our prayer lives. If we're not careful, we end up doing the same thing over and over, saying the same thing over and over. "Dear God, thank you for this day. Please help me do X, please give me Y, and please show me Z. In the name of Jesus, amen."

That's not how Anna prayed. She mixed things up. For one thing, she was a woman of worship. As she ministered in the temple courts each day, she praised God for His character. She proclaimed His goodness and His faithfulness. She ascribed glory *to* God, rather than always using prayer as an opportunity to gain something *from* God.

In addition, Anna incorporated fasting as part of her prayer life. As we saw with Esther, fasting is choosing to deny something you need in the physical realm so that you can concentrate on greater needs and greater desires in the spiritual realm. That was Anna—she chose to regularly forego the temporary pleasure and sustenance of food so that she could plead with God about her great need for salvation. For healing in her life and in the lives of her people. For rescue from the evils around her.

Finally, notice the *discipline* of Anna's prayer life. She prayed on a schedule—"night and day," according to the text. She was intentional about making prayer a priority so that her actions reflected that priority. She had the kind of internal discipline that drives many successful people to order their lives according to what they want, rather than allowing the chaos of life to push them around like boats tossed back and forth by the wind and the waves.

Yes, there is a lot we can imitate about Anna's discipline in prayer, the diversity of her methods during prayer, and her persistence in reaching out to the Lord daily over a period of not just years, but decades.

Let's pause for a moment here. Because one of the questions we need to ask when we read about Anna is this: What was she praying for all those years? As we've seen, "She never left the temple but worshiped night and day, fasting and praying" (v. 37). But what was the focus of her worship and fasting and praying?

In other words, what did she want?

I believe Anna was focused on the Messiah. She was praying for a savior, not only for herself but for her people—and for the world.

The Old Testament scriptures are filled with prophecies pointing forward to the Messiah—to the one who could come as a second Moses and lead God's people out of slavery. All the way back in Genesis when God spoke to Abraham, He said, "I will bless those who bless you, and whoever curses you I will curse; and all peoples on earth will be blessed through you" (Gen. 12:3). That's a big promise.

Later, God made a similar promise to David: "When

your days are over and you rest with your ancestors, I will raise up your offspring to succeed you, your own flesh and blood, and I will establish his kingdom. He is the one who will build a house for my Name, and I will establish the throne of his kingdom forever. I will be his father, and he will be my son" (2 Sam. 7:12–14). *Forever* is a big word.

And then in Malachi 4, the very last chapter in what we refer to as the Old Testament, God declared:

> "Surely the day is coming; it will burn like a furnace. All the arrogant and every evil-doer will be stubble, and the day that is coming will set them on fire," says the Lord Almighty. "Not a root or a branch will be left to them. But for you who revere my name, the sun of righteousness will rise with healing in its rays. And you will go out and frolic like well-fed calves. Then you will trample on the wicked; they will be ashes under the soles of your feet on the day when I act," says the Lord Almighty. (vv. 1–3)

Those are just a few of the ancient promises that point forward to a future savior. Anna was familiar with all of them. Her people knew these Scriptures and meditated on them. They clung to those promises even as Rome bound them in shackles and pressed them down into the dirt of their own land.

That's why Anna dedicated her life to prayer. Because she was desperate to see "that day coming." She longed for "the sun of righteousness" to rise "with healing in its rays." More than anything else, she wanted to be among her people when they ran out into the streets to dance and frolic "like well-fed calves."

She wanted to experience the joy of salvation. And so she prayed.

What about you? Where do you currently need rescuing? In what areas of life do you feel enslaved or pressed down? Where are you crying out for salvation?

God Keeps His Promises

As we near the end of this book about prayer, I would be remiss if I failed to mention that *connection* to God is one of the prerequisites of prayer. In order to communicate with God, you must have a connection to Him—you must know Him and be known by Him.

Think of it this way: trying to pray without any connection to God is like trying to make a phone call without any cell service. You can go through the motions of scrolling through your contacts and dialing in different numbers. You can even speak into the phone and imagine that someone out there is hearing whatever you say. But if there's no cell service—if there's no connection between you and the person you're trying to call—then your efforts are useless.

So, my sister, let me ask: do you have a connection with God?

The Bible says that in our natural state, human beings are separated from God. We are cut off. No signal. Why? Because God is perfect and we are not. Because God is holy and we are sinful. According to the apostle Paul, "all have sinned and fall short of the glory of God" (Rom. 3:23). Not only that, "the wages of sin is death" (6:23). The emphasis of that verse is not just physical death, but spiritual death. Separation from God. No service.

The good news of the gospel says there is a solution to that separation. Our service can be restored. How? Through Jesus Christ. Through a personal connection with Jesus Christ, who "takes away the sin of the world" (John 1:29). Jesus is God in the flesh who came to humanity in order to reconnect humanity with God.

And wouldn't you know it—Jesus is the baby Anna held in her arms after more than sixty years of praying for God's salvation. For rescue. For a savior. Coming up to Mary and Joseph, Jesus' parents, Anna "gave thanks to God and spoke about the child to all who were looking forward to the redemption of Jerusalem" (Luke 2:38).

Imagine the joy Anna felt in that moment. Imagine her wonder as she saw a world's worth of hope contained in that tiny hand. Did she think back to everything her father had taught her about Moses? About rescue and redemption and God's power to save? I think so.

That moment is proof that God is faithful in keeping His promises—especially when God's people pray. Anna had been praying and fasting and worshiping for decades because she was desperate for salvation. She was desperate for God to fulfill His promise of a Savior. And God was faithful to answer.

The incredible news in all of this is that God has also promised to answer our prayers. Speaking through the prophet Isaiah, He said, "Before they call I will answer; while they are still speaking I will hear" (Isa. 65:24). Speaking through the apostle John, He promised: "This is the confidence we have in approaching God: that if we ask anything according to his will, he hears us. And if we know that he hears us—whatever we ask—we know that we have what we asked of him" (1 John 5:14–15).

When you cry out to God for salvation, He hears you. When you call out to God for peace in the midst of a world in turmoil, He hears you. When you plead with God for love and warmth and tenderness because you are lonely and afraid, He hears you. When you grab hold of God's feet and refuse to let go, as the Shunammite woman did, He will not try to kick you loose; He will hear you.

Whenever you pray, God will hear you. And He will answer.

That's the promise women can rely on when they pray. That's the power women can access when they pray—that connection with Almighty God. That's the wonder and the joy women can experience when they speak with God and then listen for His response, because He does answer.

Therefore, pray. Because when women pray, God answers—and people find salvation.

Conclusion

Iwill end this book at the lap of my maternal grandmother. She was a sharecropper, along with my
grandfather, and raised fifteen children through the
Great Depression. She faced every imaginable dis-
advantage associated with the times and the racial
complexities of our country's dysfunctional past. My
earliest memory of her was during my preschool years,
when we made the annual pilgrimage from West Vir-
ginia to the South to reacquaint ourselves with our
culture, share our family stories, and just touch base
with our Southern relatives. On this particular occa-
sion, she was sitting in an old wooden rocking chair
in her modest living room just off the red clay road
that lead to her home.

We met at the intersection of my beginning and

her ending. I'm sure I was too young to fully grasp that those moments would leave an indelible impression and an inextinguishable awareness of who I was as well. I didn't yet realize that her life was coasting toward a finale. I laid my head in her lap, appreciating the moments with her, trying to draw from her deep settled eyes and old-time colloquialisms wisdom that would shape my life. I remember that an ornate, old-fashioned quilt covered her lap. I still remember the feeling of the knotted fabric where fragments of curtains, old dresses, and slacks had been cut and carefully sewn together to form a beautiful but simply done covering for her aching knees.

In the center of her lap was a huge Bible with print that was big enough to accommodate her failing sight. It was the kind of Bible that most people would place on a coffee table or a mantelpiece. The Bible was full of clippings, family pictures, notes, and other treasures.

Susie Williams Patton was my mother's mother. She had served for years as a missionary at Morning Star Baptist Church in Marion, Alabama. Her years of teaching Sunday school, delivering babies, helping the infirm, and aiding those who were in need had taken its toll. But the quilt over her knees gave comfort to the arthritis in her bones. And her brightly lit eyes and whimsical gray hair framed her leathery brown skin in such a way that she looked to me like a black *Mona Lisa.*

Like my grandmother's quilt, I've come to realize that women are varied pieces of fabric, neither monolithic nor monochromatic. Each woman comes with her own history, much like the women we have studied in this book. To rob them of their unique stories for the sake of conformity would ruin the authenticity of the narratives they share. Similarly, the women in this book are not neighbors or even from the same era. Their stories span thousands of years. They have different ethnic influences, unique experiences, and various ranges of influence. But the thread that binds them together into a quilt that warms the heart is the thread of faith and prayer. That thread unites their stories and creates a common power.

Please do not forsake your own uniqueness to live up to what others expect from you. Faith doesn't need uniformity to be effective. Instead, my sisters, walk your path, have your say, and follow your dream! Raise children or not, marry your companions or live alone, matriculate to the highest level of an Ivy League school or drive an eighteen-wheeler across the country. God doesn't need to synthetically produce you to make you a force to be reckoned with. Instead, you are a designer's original, with custom interior and endless potential. I believe that He will use your journey as a source of warmth and comfort for this cold and often lonely world.

Your faith will shape each piece of your life. It will stitch together the ragged edges of past mistakes as well as knit and weave your accomplishments and future conquests. Just know that you and God are enough to withstand the wind-chilled nights of life. As long as you rest in fidelity to His Word and resist the limitations pressed upon you by doubting Thomases that underestimate your value, you will always rise undaunted!

Understand that the rich treasure of your heritage has so equipped you that victory is in your bones. The pulse of many survivalists surround the very cells of your existence.

You are making up the portrait of the unimaginable possibilities your descendants will deem attainable. Your children's children will be influenced by their glimpse of your life and story. And so I advise you to allow the legacy of greatness to continue through you to reach others. In those inevitable moments of painful uncertainty, realize that all of these women in the Bible are your sister soldiers, your ancestral antiquities. Curate their stories, draw down their strength, and keep it moving.

Conclusion

In short, each of these amazing biblical women are your grandmothers of faith. Their DNA exists in you. Their courage runs through your veins like blood. And when life gets tough and the nights seem cold, always look back at them—always look up at their God and believe that He who has begun a good work in you shall guide you through as He did them! Until your journey brings you to the rhythm of my grandmother's rocking chair, understand that the God of all comfort and grace is the guide and the routing system that will help you finish your race.

In the words of the late Aretha Franklin, "Rock steady!" You are my sisters, aunties, grandmothers, daughters, and wives, and I love you. Rock the boardrooms, the courtrooms, the classrooms, and every room you walk into. Rock to the rhythm of your dreams and carry God's Word in your lap.

One day your grandchildren will lay their heads in your lap and stare with amazement at how you made it over! Until then, may He who started you finish His masterpiece, stitching you together for His ultimate purpose!

Notes

Introduction

1. "Some of Her Favorite Prayers," motherteresa.org, https://www.motherteresa.org/her-favorite-prayers.html, accessed March 23, 2020.

2. Sources for Mother Teresa's life and daily routine: Dick Durbin, "A Day with Mother Teresa, Huffington Post (December 6, 2017), https://www.huffpost.com/entry/a-day-with-mother-teresa_b_11914914; Sean Callahan, "Songs in the Darkness: Mother Teresa's Inner Strength," Beliefnet, https://www.beliefnet.com/faiths/catholic/2007/09/songs-in-the-darkness-mother-teresas-inner-strength.aspx.

3. Lynn Okura, "The One Thing Maya Angelou Knows for Sure," Huffington Post (September 17, 2013), https://www.huffpost.com/entry/maya-angelou-and-oprah_n_3936740.

Notes

Chapter 2

1. Erika Edwards, "African Americans 'Disproportionately Affected' by Coronavirus, CDC Report Finds," NBC News, April 8, 2020, https://www.nbcnews.com/health/health-news/african-americans-disproportionately-affected-coronavirus-cdc-report-finds-n1179306.

Chapter 3

1. C. S. Lewis, *The Complete Chronicles of Narnia* (New York: HarperCollins, 1998), p. 60.

Chapter 4

1. Rich Robinson, "The Tallit and Tzitzit," Jews for Jesus (January 9, 1994), accessed March 31, 2020, https://jewsforjesus.org/publications/newsletter/newsletter-sep-1993/the-tallit-and-tzitzit.

Chapter 8

1. "Criminal Justice Fact Sheet," NAACP, https://www.naacp.org/criminal-justice-fact-sheet.

Chapter 10

1. Terry Fitzpatrick, "Shocking Statistics, Encouraging Commitments at United Nations," FreetheSlaves.net, September 21, 2017, https://www.freetheslaves.net/shocking-statistics-encouraging-commitments-at-united-nations.

About the Author

T. D. Jakes is the #1 *New York Times* bestselling author of more than forty books and is the CEO of TDJ Enterprises, LLP. His television ministry program, *The Potter's Touch*, is watched by 3.3 million viewers every week. He has produced Grammy Award–winning music as well as hit films such as *Heaven Is for Real*, *Miracles from Heaven*, and *Jumping the Broom*. A master communicator, he hosts MegaFest, Woman Thou Art Loosed, and other conferences attended by tens of thousands. He lives in Dallas, Texas.